MW00641515

SAME TEAM

God's Playbook for Your Marriage

Same Team Credits

Copyright © 2012. All right reserved
Cover design by Blackstone Media Group
Edit and layout design by Blackstone Media Group

All Scripture quotations used in this book are taken from the Holy Bible, using either:

New King James Version (NKJV)
Copyright © 1982 by Thomas Nelson, Inc.

The Message (MSG).
Copyright © 1993, 1994, 1995, 1996, 2000, 2001, 2002 by Eugene H. Peterson.

New Living Translation (NLT)
Holy Bible. New Living Translation copyright © 1996, 2004, 2007 by Tyndale House Foundation. Used by permission of Tyndale House Publishers Inc., Carol Stream, Illinois 60188. All rights reserved.

New International Version (NIV).
Holy Bible, New International Version®, NIV ® Copyright © 1973, 1978, 1984, 2011 by Biblica, Inc. ® Used by permission. All rights reserved worldwide.

Amplified Bible (AMP)
Copyright © 1954, 1958, 1962, 1964, 1965, 1987 by The Lockman Foundation.

ISBN 978-0-9825818-1-0   Printed in the USA

Dedication

We dedicate this book to our children, Madelyn, Samantha and Jacob. We pray for your first round draft picks to start you on the Same Team.

Acknowledgments

We are thankful to our parents, Angelo and Mary Diaz and Ernie and Sandy Denker, for their examples of staying together for better and worse, richer and poorer, in sickness and in health and 'till death do us part.

We also thank Pastors Stephan Tchividjian, Reuben Ramsaran, Fidel Gomez, Doug Sauder, Jeff Denis, Greg Anderson, John Chinnelly, Steve Williams, Greg Howard, Charlie Halleran, Gennarino DeStefano, Geoff Buck, and Senior Pastor Bob Coy at Calvary Chapel Fort Lauderdale for teaching us how to succeed in marriage through the trials of life and inspiring us to teach others.

Forward

Marriage is not easy. It can be one of the most rewarding experiences in any person's life, but it can also be the source for some of life's greatest frustrations. In today's society, statistics are that almost half of all marriages will end in divorce. Even the most wonderful marriages that last 20 or 50 years will experience difficult times. Great, long-lasting marriages require a "game plan" – they do not just occur by luck or good fortune. Successful marriages are the result of many small intentional actions.

During the past decade, Mike and Angel Denker have invested an enormous amount of time to help save, improve, and strengthen an incredible number of marriages. This book provides the framework and principles they utilize to help guide and counsel couples. It gives you a plan to make your marriage successful. Throughout the chapters you will see stories and case studies of couples Mike and Angel have worked with over the years.

You will really enjoy two instinctive aspects of this book. First, all of the guidance provided throughout the book is rooted in Biblical principles. Mike and Angel are a wonderful Christian couple, and their advice and insights are based upon the standards God has set out for successful marriages. They are passionate about marriage and helping couples. Second, the book is structured in a very unique format – correlating the many aspects of marriage to the game of football – with teamwork, penalties, game-planning, etc. The book also emphasizes the strong need for a good coach to help along the way.

I have had the pleasure of knowing Mike and Angel both professionally and personally for over eight years. My wife and I have directly benefited from working with them in small group and one-on-one sessions. The wisdom and Godly teaching they have brought into our lives (and hundreds of other couples) has been amazing.

This book is a great resource for married couples to utilize throughout their life-long journey together. May your marriage be blessed.

TABLE OF CONTENTS

The Same Team Concept

The one man team is a complete and total myth.

—*Don Shula*

There's less than two minutes left in the game and our team is down by six points. We need a touchdown—quick. Our captain takes control of the huddle. We have two of the best wide receivers in the league. Everyone is confident. As the quarterback barks out the signals from behind the center, he realizes they are going to blitz him straight up the middle. He tries to call an audible, but the crowd noise is deafening. He takes the snap. He drops back under heavy pressure. Just before he becomes the middle of a nine-hundred-pound sandwich, he throws the ball over the middle. Jones, the number one receiver, has his eyes locked on the ball as he enters the end zone. Smith, the other receiver, is coming in from the other side. His eyes are wide open. He knows he is about to make the game winning catch. They are the only two people in the stadium that don't see what's coming—a huge collision. Suddenly, their tight end screams, "Same Team!"

Angel and Mike are driving home from the store. Mike says, "I think I am going to start eating eggs for breakfast." Angel replies, "It would help us lose weight if we started eating eggs for dinner." Mike agrees, "Fine, I will eat eggs for breakfast and dinner." Angel responds, "You can't eat six eggs a day, your cholesterol will go through the roof." Mike says, "I believe eggs are nature's perfect protein. I don't buy in to all the cholesterol hype." Angel responds, "You want to argue with a well-accepted fact that eggs raise cholesterol— that's stupid!" Unfortunately, this conversation is escalating out of control over a trivial point. They need to realize that the point of the conversation is lost, and more is at risk. Somebody needs to yell, "Same Team!" in order to avoid an injurious collision.

"Same Team" serves the same purpose in sports and in marriage. Don't get so wrapped up on a single issue that you risk injury to you or your teammate. That teammate is your spouse. Too many times spouses speak to one another as if they are on different teams. Your spouse is not the opponent. We have to remember that when we look at the scoreboard, we are both on the Same Team. We win or lose together.

Same Team has a husband and a wife as the players, and God as their Coach. Same Team reminds us that we have a common goal, many common interests, and a major purpose designed by God. He provided us with the playbook for marriage, the Bible. Philippians 2:2 describes Same Team as *"being like-minded, having the same love, being one in spirit and purpose."* The Bible contains the rules of the game—the Ten Commandments and the Golden Rule. The playbook is also full of promises, encouragement, praise, and hundreds of replays from the past. The playbook shows how to win. It inspires us to stay in the game when the going gets tough. We expect to have struggles, and we expect to win because God's playbook promises both.

What does being on a team have to do with marriage? Everything. The dictionary defines a team as "a number of persons associated together in work or activity." It can also be a group on the same side as in football or debate. Marriage is two people of the opposite sex united as husband and wife in a consensual and contractual relationship recognized by law. A more relaxed definition states that marriage is an intimate or close union. Merging these terms, you have a bond of like ideas involving two people who are working together in an ongoing relationship. All teams and marriages have a beginning. Notice there is no time limit or ending. This is symbolized by the circle of the wedding ring having no end. When you join a team, you may be recruited, elected, or volunteer. When you marry, you give up your "free agency" status in exchange for lifelong loyalty to a team. How you define it and who is allowed on your team determines the outcome or success of the relationship.

Your team begins with the two of you. Even with all your newly combined skills, gifts, and abilities, it's not enough to make your marriage a winner. There is a way to succeed in marriage that has worked for thousands of years—having God as your Head Coach. God has unlimited capacity. He is able to do more than what we can accomplish in our human ability. He can do miracles. When we make a conscious decision to invite Him to be the head of our team, we request His power to affect situations that we have no control over.

The first time I heard God call a play for Angel and me was in 1997, our first season together. We had been going to church together for several weeks. We were dating. At the end of every church service, the pastor gave an open invitation to start a personal relationship with Jesus. At the end of every service, I would say the same prayer, "God, if she goes, I'll go. If she goes, I'll go." Jesus was knocking on my heart, but I wanted Angel to go with me. This became my weekly routine.

We were attending a large church with a couple of thousand people at each service. I noticed another routine in addition to my own. At the end of every service and before the pastor gave an invitation, hundreds of people would zip up the covers on their Bibles. The harmonious zipping became my cue to start praying, "God, if she goes, I'll go." One night, the pastor paused. The zippers zipped. I prayed. Suddenly, I was overwhelmed with a single word: "lead!" I knew in an instant the command's meaning. I immediately got up from my seat and walked up to the front of the church.

The command was so direct; I moved before I could hesitate or second-guess my decision.

So there I was, standing alone at the front of the church within six feet of the pastor. Everything happened so fast. The pastor said, "Some of you may be wondering why this man is standing up here . . ." He proceeded to give the invitation. When he was finished, others joined me. The first person to join me was Angel. We started our journey with Jesus, together.

God called me to lead. Angel followed my lead. We were married later that year.

Being married is a challenge, especially in these times of disposable marriage. One out of two marriages breaks up before the five-year mark. Today, married couples barely withstand the everyday stress of living with another person, let alone the trials and tragedies that occur during a lifetime. What does this say about us? It should be obvious that we need God more than ever. This is especially true when many of our children are being raised by single moms, a stepparent, or cohabitating partners. The current culture has not only erased the stigma of divorce, it has embraced those who have tried and failed at marriage as if it is the new norm for our society.

Angel and I enjoy a blended family. Our children—
Maddy, Sammi, and Jake—come from my first
marriage. While growing up, they lived with their mom
most of the time. Their mom lives thirty-two miles from
our home. When we were interviewed by the pastor that
would later marry us, he responded to our situation,
"Ahh, divorced with children, the gift that keeps on
giving." If you have children from a former marriage,
you know what I'm talking about. If you don't, you have
no idea. Our goal is to make sure you never know.

Over several decades, morals have declined and truth
has become relative. Gray has replaced black and white
in our educational system. The influence of television,
the removal of prayer from the schools, women leaving
children to the care of others, and the decline of church
attendance have all had an impact on the moral fiber of
the country. We could present statistics and a valid
argument just on the removal of prayer from the
classroom. This single judicial act happened in 1962.
From that point in time, teen pregnancies have
increased, youth violence has increased, and SAT scores
have gone down.

We are not going to spend time analyzing the past.

We want to deal with the present and hope to change the future for marriage and our children. We believe that a strong marriage between a husband and wife establishes the foundation for society to thrive and prosper. Having experienced divorces, we also acknowledge that without God, marriage is doomed from the start. Think about it: two sinners and one house. Where is that going?

Marriage takes effort and grace, neither of which comes naturally. We are in a quest for an easy life. Fast food, fast cars, fast track. We are living life fast and furious, and a partner who is not keeping up is just getting in the way. Living fast leads to impatience, and impatience leads to alternative choices or apathy. These choices and attitudes can destroy relationships. When a person does not meet our needs, we may become bored or disgruntled and look to the "greener grass" rather than working on the issues and resolving disputes.

Keeping your team together starts with planning and commitment and involves ongoing training. Imagine being on a team and thinking, "I already know the drills there is no reason to train for the next game." Marriage requires care and focus. It is like a garden that can grow and flourish with proper tending or be overgrown and choked with weeds due to lack of nourishment and neglect.

Fellow teammates cry out, "Same Team" so that no one gets hurt by another member of the Same Team. Our goal in creating the Same Team concept is to preserve marriage as a partnership that treats problems as issues and not opportunities to attack each other as opponents. We are on the Same Team! We want you to keep marriage your second highest priority. God should be your first. This book will show you how to improve, enhance, and even save your marriage.

Joining a team in marriage links you together as one new entity. There are ways to tell the world you are connected to a team. When the wife assumes her husband's last name as her own, she is communicating her bond to him. They are united as Mr. and Mrs. Somebody. In football, you get a uniform with team colors and a unique logo. The married couple has the same name on their jersey and a new number, their anniversary date. Now all they need is a coach.

The concept of Same Team is to incorporate God into your team, not as a sideline player or second string but as Head Coach to lead both of you through your marriage. When you bring your problems, fears, and concerns to God, you have increased your chances of success through an infusion of supernatural power. God, the Head Coach, is always available, and His desire is to make you better.

The goal of any coach is to help you win. Winning comes with effort. The coach is the key to the success of the team but can only be effective if the players have a desire to learn, listen, and work together as a unit. The coach determines the plays that the team must carry out. The players must have their heads and hearts in the game.

God wants to have a relationship with us, and He wants us to follow His playbook, the Bible. Learning what God has to say about marriage is inspiring when we find that there are time-tested truths about this covenant relationship. Marriage is very special to God. It represents His relationship with His Son, and it represents Jesus' relationship with us. Anything this special is worth fighting for.

Our desire in writing this book is to eliminate the "D word." We don't even allow this word in our home.

Divorce breaks up the team. Divorce hurts the heart and soul of the players and the fans or family members. Divorce has a negative impact on society. We lose monetarily and emotionally. In most cases, a single parent ends up with less time and less money. Divorce has a trickle-down effect, leaving a negative impact on future generations. It erodes feelings of loyalty and breaks the bond between two people.

A broken bond violates the intimate seal, allowing other things to get through and weaken the relationship. Imagine two pieces of paper glued together and allowed to set for a while. When you try to pull them apart, they tear. Some of each piece stays stuck to the other. That is how it is with divorce. No matter how much you try to sever a relationship, there is always a piece that stays behind as baggage, a part of a broken heart, or a lost piece of your soul. Rarely do you hear someone say truthfully that their divorce was a positive thing. When the team loses, it hurts.

Loyal teams stay together through winning and losing seasons. Team loyalty in marriage means your team is number one in your life. The way you feel about your team shows in the way you train and practice. You must dedicate time and effort to learn and execute the plays.

When you take the time to learn about each other and what the Bible says about marriage, you take two giant steps toward staying together. It is an honor to be on your team. Your team should make you proud. You should enjoy the time you spend with your team. Your team is undefeatable because you have a great coach, God. You have the best leader as captain, the husband who runs great plays. You have the most enthusiastic, supportive, encouraging cheerleader, the wife. You have raving fans—kids, family, and supportive friends. When you celebrate, you go all out for the team. You train and work hard to see your team succeed. You suit up and prepare to win!

What Does Football Have to Do with Marriage?

Coming together is a beginning. Keeping together is progress. Working together is success.

—Henry Ford

Every great coach has mastered three speeches: the pre-game, the half-time, and the post-game. Every season starts with a modified pre-game. *"OK, men, last season was tough. We had some tough losses. We endured injuries. Some of the calls went against us. We are going to endure bad calls and untimely injuries every season, but we expect to win every game. I have seen our preparation on the field and in the classroom. We have what it takes to win every game this season.*

We have to remind ourselves and each other continuously, winning is expected. Victory is in our hands. We will do everything we can to secure it."

"Team" brings certain thoughts to mind. A team is a cohesive unit of two or more joined together in some activity or purpose. The team concept implies loyalty and unity. You defend your team. You stay on your team's side. You may be losing, but you stay with your team. You have camaraderie with your team. You join your team. There's no "I" in team. Team is about "us." You give it all for your team. No matter what, you have your team.

Why can't we take these concepts and apply them to our marriage? We can, and we should. In my twenties, I was a Miami Dolphins cheerleader for five years, captain for three. I knew the team concept, but I failed to apply it to my former marriage. After several years in a Christian marriage, Mike and I both learned what we had missed the first time.

Being married without God is like being on a football team without a coach. You do whatever seems best for you with little concern for the rest of your team. Without a coach, you may end up breaking rules and hurting each other unintentionally. We love football. We both grew up watching the Miami Dolphins. Our parents were die-hard Dol-fans. As a professional NFL cheerleader, it was fun to cheer and dance for the team when we were winning. It was especially fun to go to two Super Bowls. It was not fun losing both times. When your team loses, your hope starts to fade. Fear creeps in. How will we do next season? Will I still make the team?

Success breeds confidence. Failure breeds fear. It is a lot easier to be positive in a winning environment. As you and the team get closer to the goal, winning a lot more than losing, it is easier to practice and cheer. You get to the game early with a bright-eyed feeling of excitement and anticipation. After the kickoff, you start to feel how the players feel. Depending on what the scoreboard says, you're either fired up and energized, or you're hot, thirsty, tired, and ready for the locker room.

Half-time provides a new challenge of recharging and refueling your body and mind for the second half of the game, the part that will end in victory or defeat. All games are won or lost in the second half because no matter what, when time runs out, you're up, down, or even.

When you first get married, it's like pre-game and kickoff. Everything is fun, new, and exciting. You are filled with hope for the future. After the kickoff (wedding), the rest of the game is made up of plays. Each play is a success or failure. The payoff is a score. In football, keeping score is simple. There are only four ways to score: a touchdown, an extra point, a field goal, or a safety. In marriage, keeping score is complex, but victories are more frequent. You can have marriage victories every day, month, and year. Football is limited to a set number of games.

On the field, several successful plays in a row can be undone by one bad play. The same is true in our marriage. The husband gets up early. He makes the coffee. He delivers a cup of coffee made the way she likes it to his wife in bed. As she crawls out of bed and heads for the bathroom, he quickly makes the bed. This guy is on a roll. As he is fluffing his wife's pillow, she screams from the bathroom. She just sat on the cold porcelain bowl because he left the seat up last night. Fumble! Is everything lost? Is the situation hopeless?

No, the game goes on. The team has to recover. It doesn't matter who makes the next big play because both have the same goal, both are on the Same Team.

A tense situation is a good opportunity for a time-out. If it is something major, it may require a half-time talk. Marriage is made up of many games and many seasons. Unlike football, half-times can be scheduled as needed, not only after the first thirty minutes of the game. Half-time is a time to recharge and refuel physically, mentally, and spiritually before we go back out on the field.

Every football season starts with one mission—win the Super Bowl. Every decision, play, and strategy must align with the mission. If it does not lead toward the ultimate goal, it is a distraction. The team avoids these distractions by keeping the end in mind. Many couples enter into marriage with all their focus on the beginning, the wedding, with little thought to the rest of their marriage.

A couple plans a wedding. They choose a date, a ceremony, time, and place. They discuss whom to invite, what they will wear, what they will eat, the music, and the flowers. All this planning for one day.

What about the days after? How much planning has been done for their life together?

Whether you start planning before your wedding or several years into your marriage, there is always hope. Learning how to be a good partner, a kind person, a better helper, friend, and encourager will strengthen your marriage. The most important marriage bond is the one you have with God. He will keep the cord of three strands strong.

When Mike and I designed our wedding invitations, we chose a special verse, *"A cord of three strands is not quickly broken."* [1] The three parts of the cord are husband, wife, and God. Our wedding rings are made of three rings linked together. Continuous care is required to keep the cord from unraveling.

We attended our first marriage seminar six months after our wedding. Some friends asked if everything was OK. Their concern made us laugh. Maintenance avoids costly repairs. When I take my car in for an oil change, nobody thinks my car is broken. It is preventive maintenance. Our marriage is very important. We need to invest in its maintenance. The seminar was like an oil change for our marriage.

To set a good foundation, they taught us how to create a mission statement that would set the stage for beginning our life together. They gave us a couple of hours alone to come up with a mission. Mike and I started by listing our shared values:

- honesty
- faith
- God first
- work
- constant growth
- learning
- sharing ideas
- open communication
- serving each other and others

We also wrote down some goals:

Convey a hope for a future of love and peace in our family.

Prepare our children spiritually, physically, and emotionally for life's struggles and temptations.

Serve God with all our heart, mind and strength.

Set an example for others by seeking God and

following His commandments.

We've continued learning about effective goal setting. A goal requires a specific activity and a deadline. When you write a goal, you should have an action to perform and a time frame to get it done. With these guidelines, you should be able to come up with some actions to merge your goals into shared plans for your life together.

For example, we knew that to serve God with all our heart, mind, and strength, we needed to equip ourselves with the knowledge of His Word. We made a commitment to read the Bible cover to cover in a year. Although we did this independently, many couples read together. You will discover what works best for you. Learning the Word of God sets the foundation for knowing His will for your marriage.

Another step is to find marriage mentors—couples who will journey alongside you and encourage you to grow together. Our church provides small groups for married couples as well as a married couples' ministry and biblical counseling. Continue to seek sources of inspiration and guidance to continue growing together.

What would happen if after the first season a player decided they didn't need to go to practice? Can you imagine taking four or five months off from a physical activity and then trying to perform at full capacity? I can't even take a week off from the gym without feeling muscle soreness. The same thing goes with marriage. You can't ignore the relationship and expect it to flourish. You've got to pay attention.

Take some time out to pray together and discuss what God has done and is doing in your life right now. Then sit down together and write a couple of sentences about what the Holy Spirit is telling you as a team. Finally, try to simplify it into one sentence. Complete the following statement, "Our marriage exists to . . ." Make a plaque or a banner of your marriage mission statement so you can remind yourselves what God has conveyed to you. We ended up with, "Glorify God as an example that inspires stronger marriages."

Every year, revisit your mission statement by summing up the past year and how God has worked in your lives. See if your marriage is staying true to your mission statement. Adjust your goals based on how you have both grown in your spiritual walk. As you draw closer to God, your goals will become more challenging. God may call you to do new things, which you never imagined when you first got together.

Set a date to revisit your mission statement each year and set new goals. Choose a specific time, just like a business meeting. Pick a special place and bring calendars. An aggressive game plan will invigorate and reignite your passion. Consider a weekend away from it all or an anniversary celebration to recharge your minds and bodies for the year ahead.

Most of all, have fun with this. Don't make it a chore. We schedule our anniversary getaway in December to someplace cold. Living in Florida makes seeing seasonal changes a treat. We dig out sweaters in anticipation of chilly walks followed with hot cocoa by the fire. However you choose to do it, just do it! You cannot keep putting off time together. You need to work on the details that lead to a winning year.

The opposition does not want us to win. These forces are like our division rivals working and cheering against us. Besides the other teams, we have to deal with penalties, turnovers, dropped passes, poor execution, and blitzes. You can use your imagination to determine what these look like in your marriage. Regardless of the specifics, they represent challenges and setbacks that make our marriages an adventure. During some of these challenges, you get your uniform dirty. You may have fights in the huddle—disagreements on the next play. You can lose focus of the goal.

Just like games are broken up into quarters, our marriages go through seasons. The Miami Dolphins represent the spectrum of success and failure. In 1972, seventeen wins, no losses. In 2007, one win, fifteen losses. Regardless of their record, the Dolphins stayed together, made adjustments, and looked forward to the next season.

The seasons in marriage are marked by many different events. They include before kids, full house, empty nest, good job, bad job, no job, dependent parents, transfers, moves, and a long list of others. Regardless of season, thousands of marriages have thrived in good times and bad because they remind themselves they are on the Same Team. They know the team is bigger than the individual players. You should be able to be positive during any season knowing the best is in front of you. Regardless of how it looks right now, there is always hope. Getting through the tough times is what makes the team stronger and resilient. When we overcome a great challenge together with our favorite person in the whole wide world, it's like winning in overtime. When the ball crosses that goal line, it is sweet victory.

Who Exactly Is on My Team?

Build for your team a feeling of oneness, of
dependence on one another and of strength to be
derived by unity.

—Vince Lombardi

It was raining cats and dogs. We were driving from the hotel to Walt Disney World. I had a great idea. We stopped at a souvenir store on the way and bought yellow rain ponchos. I told Angel that we would stand out in the huge crowds of visitors at Disney. The bright yellow ponchos would make it easy for us to keep track of the kids. As we entered the gate and approached Main Street, we witnessed thousands of people wearing the identical yellow poncho with Mickey Mouse on the back.

Uniforms are important. They identify who we are, but they have to give us a unique identity to be effective.

Team colors create unity, and fans adopt ways to wear them, whether on their bodies as clothing or paint on their faces or chests. Our son, Jake, is a fanatic for his teams. He loves green with orange, but he considers blue with orange offensive. Even though different players have different positions, they still wear the same colors, share the same team name, and the same goals. These unique identifiers indicate who is for you and who is against you. Each player has to understand and perform at their positions.

Eve was created for Adam because Adam was not sufficient unto himself. He needed a *"helper."*[2] It is interesting to note that Eve came from his side—not above or below. We encourage you to read Genesis 2 because it reveals that God sees us as equal partners with different responsibilities just as the coach sees each player. The man is to lead, provide, and protect. The woman is to help him and bear the children.

Today, many women are doing part of the man's assignment, and many men are doing part of the woman's role. This is out of God's order. Can you imagine if the center decided to become a wide receiver because he did not like how the wide receiver was playing his position? It doesn't work in football, and it doesn't work in marriage.

When you first marry, you may think that it is just the two of you, husband and wife. Then reality sets in. You find that your parents, stepkids, or even close friends seem to be part of your team. All these people may influence your team, but you need to have a separateness that is you, your spouse, and God. Without this core team, the others suffer. If you are not "one with your spouse," then you will become influenced in decisions that affect both of you by someone who is not part of your team. This endangers the sanctity of your team. Your parents are their own team. That is why the Bible says to leave, cleave, and make your own family. Your friends have their own families. The only people who are part of your team are your spouse and your children, and the kids are playing for you.

The role children play should not be "influencer." You are supposed to influence your children, not the other way around. Many couples allow their lives to be ruled by toddlers and young children. Positions on the team have not been established. A child needs to see your team working together from day one. They are supposed to come to you for guidance. Learn God's commandments and teach them to your children. *"Impress them on your children. Talk about them when you sit at home and when you walk along the road, when you lie down and when you get up."* [3]

Your children rely on the strength of your marriage for security. When you are on a commercial jet with children, they go over the emergency instructions. They say, "If the oxygen masks come down, put yours on first. Then assist your children with their masks." As a parent, this would seem odd to you, but if you can't breathe, you can't help anyone else. If you keep your marriage strong, your children will gain strength from it. The marriage has to be the most important human relationship on the team.

Once we put our children in a close second to our marriage, we have to set clear boundaries for outsiders, especially our parents. Sometimes I wish a referee would walk in from the kitchen, blow his whistle, and stop play. The referee would alert our family and friends after the screech of the whistle halts all activity, "Offsides . . . Mike's mom . . . pushing opinion too hard on Angel . . . Mom offers no opinions for five days, and that's a first down."

In marriage, "offsides" means you entered into another team's zone. In football, this causes the play to be repeated but with a loss of yardage. In marriage, you may have much higher consequences if you side with a parent or a child against your spouse. When someone is pulling you over to a side that is not in line with your spouse, you need to stop and review the action you are about to take. Consideration means you take into account the other person's views and feelings. The antonym is boneheaded move. Make the right play, spouse first in every situation on the Same Team. In our marriage, I stop, pray, and ask, "How does God want me to treat his daughter?" When God considers my wife His daughter, I'm the son-in-law.

Speaking of in-laws, some are well meaning. Some are meddlesome. You need to consider your spouse and act with them as your focus. This is how we all want to be treated when we choose our mate. We want to be number one to our favorite person in the whole wide world. I get along great with Angel's mom, but I have been reminded of my place in her world.

While having dinner with my mother-in-law and

some of Angel's cousins, Angel's mom started to complain about her sons. All the issues were trivial. During the conversation, I broke an unwritten rule. I made a comment in agreement with my mother-in-law regarding one of her sons. She pointed her finger at me and said, "Mike, watch your tongue. You're not blood." She made a great point. I'm not on her team. She's not on my team. We joke from time to time during family discussions. "Be careful! You're not blood." Our home team is Angel and I . . . 'til death do us part.

Why do we allow time and familiarity to erode this important factor of marriage? We need to stay alert and aware of the outside influences that distract us and divert our attention. We have to continue to remind ourselves to stay "other-focused." The most important "other" in your life is your spouse.

Children are the greatest asset to a married couple; however, some couples allow their priorities to get out of whack. Many women forget they have a husband when a baby comes into the home. Many men feel forgotten or unloved as they vie for their wife's attention and compete with an infant. Unfaithfulness has frequently occurred when a spouse feels neglected or unimportant. Children can take up energy and time, leaving wives tired and uninterested in sex or unavailable for communication. This is when it is even more important to establish ways to be together emotionally, physically, and spiritually. Couples that realize this are better equipped to cope with the early years of child rearing.

The last thing that should come between you is the children you created. Make time to discuss the children when they are not around. Get on the same page so that they do not throw you off your game. You may find parenting a trying experience, but once you learn some simple techniques, you are ready for most situations.

We have three children. Angel is a stepmom and a strict disciplinarian for how the house should run. I am strict about dress, friends, and what the kids are allowed to do. If we are not in alignment, we will end up arguing when the kids are around. Since the children are already living through the consequences of divorce, it is important for us to show them stability and security. In order for them to feel secure, they must know that the marriage is secure.

Friends and coworkers are great to have. They help

us. We have fun together. We share significant parts of our lives with each other. They are an integral part of our community and support system. They are not on our team.

Angel and I prioritize our relationships. First, we each have a personal relationship with God through Jesus Christ. The second most important relationship is our marriage. Our children are close behind. That's our team. We also prioritize our supporters—family, friends, coworkers, community. As we plan our time and how to invest it, we rely on our priorities. We ask each other, "Based upon our priorities and our goals for our team, what is the best thing for us to do?"

When we are on the Same Team, we do not allow intruders on our turf, we protect each other, and we take directions from our Head Coach and His playbook. He also provides training and drills. They develop the skills we need to reach the goal. We are there for each other to fight against the enemy. The critical skills in marriage require practice—praying, aligning with God's will, adhering to and practicing His commandments, and learning new ways to strengthen our team.

Although many people may think they are helping you by involving themselves in your team, God has joined you together as one with each other and no one else. Your kids will grow up, your parents will grow old, and your friends will change. Allow God to keep the two of you in harmony for life. Choose to receive this blessing. Cherish it. Nurture it. Protect it.

The Penalty: Broken Trust

The Play: Bianca and Steve

Bianca and Steve have been married a little over a year. Bianca is very close to her mother and talks with her daily on the phone. On the weekends, they usually go to her parents' home for dinner. One Sunday afternoon, as the dishes were being cleared from the table, Steve overheard his mother-in-law whisper to his wife, "Has his boss given him any more trouble about the sales results?" Bianca shook her head to her mom as if to say, "Don't mention this right now." Steve started to steam because her mom knew about his personal work issues. On the ride home, he blew up in the car saying, "I can't believe you blabbed to your mom about my job. Now she'll tell the whole town, if she hasn't already, about my work problems. Can't you just keep your trap shut about things that involve me?"

Bianca's temper got her going when she heard his remarks. She fired back without hesitation, "My mom is my best friend. I tell her everything. She's not going to tell anybody important, so why are you being so paranoid?" Steve became animated. "Paranoid? Why is it that we can't live our lives without your mom knowing every intimate detail? I'm supposed to be your best friend, remember, 'Leave and cleave.' You need to cut the cord and think of my feelings before you tell anyone anything when it comes to our personal business."

Bianca started to become emotional, and she could feel tears forming. "Steve, I didn't realize that this was a sore subject. I'm not sure what I should and shouldn't say to my mom. I'm used to telling her everything. Maybe we can talk about it, and I can understand better." Steve said, "You should just have common sense about this. A man needs to be respected, and I don't know how to teach you this. Let's just agree that from now on you don't mention me to her unless you've spoken to me about it first. Keep my name out of your conversations." Bianca thought to herself this will be impossible because

Steve is the main topic most of the time. She decided to be quiet and hoped this whole thing would die down.

Coach to Steve:

Although Steve's premise of *"leave and cleave"* may be correct in principle, his delivery and context leave a lot to be desired. Have you ever wondered why "response" is the root of "responsibility"? Our responses indicate our grace and maturity. *A soft answer turns away wrath.* Steve is embarrassed by his situation at work. In tough times, Steve needs to reinforce his prayer life and dedicate daily time to reading his Bible. This extra effort will remind him (and make it believable) to *be anxious for nothing. Steve can bring all his requests to God so that the peace of God will protect Steve's heart and mind.* If Steve trusts that God *plans to prosper you and not to harm you, plans to give you hope and a future,* he will replace his embarrassment with hope. He will exchange an animated answer with a grace-filled acknowledgment.

Steve also wants to avoid intentionally grounding the mother-daughter relationship that helped make Bianca the woman he chose above all others. Steve's edict to his wife regarding potential topics of conversation is ridiculous and impossible for her to maintain. If Bianca was bragging about him, he would be thinking, "Don't stop, baby. You're on a roll!" Steve's vision is blurred like so many referees throwing a flag before they are sure what happened. He needs to step back and allow the Holy Spirit to work things out in Bianca's heart. She will speak, *not in words taught us by human wisdom but in words taught by the Spirit,* fortified with discernment. As the leader, provider, and protector of the family, the man is going to endure tough times. We need to dig down deep like an offensive line on third and nine in the fourth quarter with the game on the line. We need to *let our light our shine* in the darkness and inspire our wives and families with hope and strength regardless of the circumstances. *We are ambassadors for Christ,* sons of the Lord Most High, *and we know that all things work together for good to those who love God, to those who are the called according to His purpose.*

Playbook for Steve:

Genesis KJV 2:24, Proverbs 15:1, Philippians 4:6, Jeremiah 29:11 NIV, 1 Corinthians 2:13 NIV, Matthew 5:16, 2 Corinthians 5:20, Romans 8:28

Coach to Bianca:

When Steve mentioned *"leave and cleave"* to Bianca, he had a good point. Many marriages get outside interference from the sidelines or in-laws, and if one spouse is closer to their parents than the other, the other spouse can feel left out. It is not good for one spouse to talk behind the other's back, even to their own mother. It divides and disrupts the sanctity of their marriage. It betrays a confidence shared between the two. What seems to be an innocent exchange of events turns into gossip. *The tongue is a small part of the body* that can do tons of damage in relationships. *If we could control our tongues, we would be perfect and could also control ourselves in every other way.* Gossip can be merely talking about someone when they are not present, true or untrue. To avoid gossip, remember the acronym *THINK*. Use this test before speaking. *T* is it true? *H*—is it helpful? *I*—is it inspiring? *N*—is it necessary? *K*—is it kind?

Bianca can employ the THINK test to determine if she should share something about Steve with her mother or anyone else. When we talk about our spouse in their absence, it should be to praise and honor them to others. Many people today practice what they call "male" or "wife bashing" as comic relief with their friends. This is dangerous to marriage. *Fire goes out without wood, and quarrels disappear when gossip stops.* Bianca can speak to her mom about her life without sharing Steve's personal struggles. She can ask her mom to pray for Steve's work to be productive and successful. Bianca's venting to her mom is not helpful to Steve. Sometimes women give unnecessary details and make things worse. As wives, we should never share anything that would hurt our husbands or display a lack of confidence in them. We are to protect our husband's character at all times. Is it helpful and inspiring for Bianca to give the details? It's definitely not necessary. *Tell God what you need, and thank him for all he has done. Then you will experience God's peace, which exceeds anything we can understand.* Wives should be in daily prayer for their husbands and their work. *As soon as I pray, You answer me; You encourage me by giving me strength.* You can't be on the Same Team sharing secret conversations with players from another team.

Playbook for Bianca:

Genesis KJV 2:24, James 3:5 NIV, James 3:2 NLT, Proverbs 26:20 NLT, Philippians 4:6 NLT, Psalms 138:3 NLT

Helping Each Other—
Assist on the Play

*The best teams have chemistry. They communicate
with each other, and they sacrifice personal glory
for the common goal.*

—Dave DeBusschere

The quarterback takes the snap. His favorite wide
receiver makes a move on the defender and sprints up
the right sideline. The quarterback realizes he is being
blitzed. He throws the ball to the right sideline about
twenty-five yards downfield. The receiver suddenly
stops and pivots to his right. As he turns, the ball lands
in his hands. The referee runs toward him signaling a
completion. The crowd goes crazy. The announcers
cannot believe what they are seeing:

"Wow, did you see that! The ball was in the air long before the receiver ever turned around."

"Yeah, the receiver turned with all the confidence in the world that the ball would be there right on time."

"That's amazing chemistry."

Every quarterback needs a favorite wide receiver. When he's under pressure or the game is on the line, he is going to throw to his favorite. He has confidence in his favorite. He knows his abilities, his habits, and his timing. They have chemistry.

Was this chemistry there on the day they met? Was their timing in perfect sync the first time they practiced together? Probably not. Where did they get that chemistry? They worked on it. They practiced every day with the team. Then they stayed late practicing together until their timing and anticipation were perfect.

When Mike and I first got together, we had some chemistry. Our physical attraction for each other was a start, but great chemistry develops with time and effort. The first time Mike saw the books on my bookshelf, he told me that he had read several of the same books and many were on his bookshelf. Immediately, I felt the connection between us grow.

In addition to books and looks, we grew together in our worldviews, our perceptions, our goals, our dreams, our habits, our strengths, and our weaknesses.

We refer to each other as "my favorite person in the whole wide world." This conjures up the thought that out of billions of people on the earth, Mike chose me, and I picked him. It's not just physical; we're best friends. Being called their favorite person in the whole wide world gives you a sense of security and loyalty. It is so cool to think that you are someone else's favorite person. It makes you feel special. We all want to feel special to someone, especially the person with whom we have chosen to spend our life.

That "specialness" is what makes us a team. It's the unique traits we each bring to the game. Teams have people with different skill sets. Some players run faster, others can catch or throw well. Some are accurate at kicking the ball. Teammates look different. A player who tackles or guards is usually beefy compared to one who is running down the field. How these differences combine either makes or breaks the team.

In our first year of marriage, I noticed Angel writing

on some lines printed at the bottom of our bank statement. I never noticed those lines before. I had no idea of their purpose. Angel explained you need them to balance your checkbook to the penny. I was instantly blown away by the intelligence and attention to detail of my new wife.

Each spouse enters the marriage team with different sets of skills. This is important to the vitality of the marriage. If each spouse has the same exact skills, one is obsolete. These differences are to be cherished and celebrated. Our personalities sometimes blend well together and other times cause friction depending on how they are expressed. When I react negatively to Angel, it can cause arguments and hurt feelings. In football, a strong team is made up of players who are more concerned about the success of the team than individual accomplishments. I strive to respond to Angel with honor and understanding in an effort to strengthen our team.

When I fail to honor her, mercy and grace are required. We all screw up. Everyone fails sooner or later. After you have said or done something hurtful to your spouse, ask for forgiveness in a timely manner. It's a game changer. If you have been wronged, *"do not let the sun go down on your anger."* [4] Forgive your favorite person in the whole wide world. Unforgiveness leads to anger to resentment to bitterness. Bitterness can grow like a cancer that eats away at your relationship.

When we join together for a lifetime with a person, no matter how well we understand each other and get along, there are times that you will not agree. Circumstances will take you by surprise. Your chemistry will determine how you weather the storms. Emotions, tempers, and attitudes can put out the flames of passion quickly. This is why it's important to get to know each other as friends who can work together through a problem.

How do we improve chemistry? It is a combination of timing, talent, and trust. First, we have to make the time, or more frequently, take the time from another activity. Your marriage has to be a priority in your daily routine and your weekly schedule. Second, assess your mutual and unique talents and make a list. The list has three columns—his, hers, and ours. These three columns are pillars that sustain your relationship and make your marriage more powerful than the sum of its parts. What does that mean?

In nature, two forces come together to create a greater single force. There's an old story from the county fair. Powerful horses competed for the blue ribbon by pulling large amounts of weight over a short distance. After several efforts, a horse was awarded the blue ribbon for pulling 4,600 pounds. The second place horse pulled 4,500 pounds. Logic dictates that the two, together, would pull 9,100 pounds. When they hitched the two horses as a team, something miraculous happened. The two horses pulled over 12,000 pounds.

This same phenomenon is true in marriage. When husband and wife team up with good chemistry, great things can be accomplished when both are working toward the same goal.

The most important ingredient in chemistry is trust. On the wedding day, there is trust. Trust, however, can be lost in a moment, but it can only be restored over time. I test this truth all the time. I come home late without calling for the fifth time in a month. I say I'm sorry. Angel forgives me every time, but it erodes Angel's trust that I will be somewhere when I say I will. Every time this happens, I want everything to go back to normal as soon as I say I'm sorry. It usually doesn't, and I get disappointed. Disappointment leads to anger. Anger leads to . . . somebody yell, "Same Team!"

Every time we injure trust, it takes a little longer to recover. It's the same way with a sprained ankle. The first time I sprained my ankle, I rubbed it, moved my foot around, and went back to playing. The fourth sprain sent me home with an ice pack. The last time I sprained my ankle, I could not walk for over a week. Your ankle gets injured easier and easier when it's aggravated, and recovery takes longer and longer. Trust and ankles have a lot in common.

Have you ever had someone offer help on a project? Sometimes they have no clue, or they try to do it the "easy way" and not necessarily the right way. Although their intentions are good, this kind of helper does not suit you. It's the wrong kind of helper. A person who approaches life differently from the way you do may not be the best choice for a mate. We learn from magnets opposites attract, but if they come together the wrong way, they repel. How do we deal with this paradox? Magnets only work when they come together the right way. Our attitude and our beliefs dictate how we come together as a couple—whether we attract or repel each other. Marriage is no different from any other important game. Winning or losing is greatly influenced by attitude.

"The LORD God said, 'It is not good for the man to be alone. I will make a helper suitable for him.'" [5] We often focus on "helper," but "suitable" is extremely important. Suitable is another way of describing chemistry. The Amplified Bible uses the words "adaptable and complementary" to describe God's helper for man. "Adaptable" means able to handle situations effectively together. "Complementary" means a positive partner, one who enhances your efforts. The dictionary says "mutually supplying each other's lack." That is exactly what you need in marriage. On the Same Team, we are making an effort to advance the team's goal. There is an understood like-mindedness. One player does not go off on their own agenda.

In preparation for the next play, the offense usually huddles. They come together to reestablish understanding and unity. Husband and wife need to huddle up every morning before they go their separate ways. Praying together is a great way to huddle up.

When you share your daily thoughts, struggles, hopes, and desires together in front of God, it provides you with strength that comes from the Holy Spirit. He is going to guide you. When we think of things that make a team, we think of each player's strengths that contribute to the success of the team. Prayer is the supernatural power that keeps your team strong.

When Angel and I pray together, we hear each other's heart. We don't interrupt each other in prayer unlike some of our conversations. We allow each other to totally express our hearts. Prayer etiquette dictates you cannot stop praying until the other person says, "Amen." Prayer is the perfect prescription for removing the heat from a hot discussion. Sometimes I silently pray for God to fix her while we are arguing. God's response is always the same. "I will fix her right after I am done fixing you."

We heard on the radio that the average couple argues 186 times a year for twenty-five minutes. That's about a half hour every other day! I'm sure this is little spats or disagreements on an issue. I listen to my kids go at it. They seem like they're fighting, and when I call them out on it, they say, "We're not fighting, we're just talking." That form of talking, where one talks over the other trying to be "righter" than the other, is the same trivial banter that leads to most arguments. How helpful is it to be constantly correcting someone? When a team member doesn't make the play, do they really need to have the negative result reinforced? Sometimes, instant replay is not a good thing. It has been said in teaching and coaching we are to look for the positive, first, before correcting or pointing out the flaws.

When training animals, positive behavior is reinforced and rewarded. We also respond positively when we are rewarded and reinforced verbally by our "favorite person in the whole wide world." We have to train our minds to see the positive and train our tongues to say encouraging words. GOD wants us to see each other through His eyes, the eyes of our perfect Father. We have a special verse that we put to good use in our home. *"Finally, brothers and sisters, whatever is true, whatever is noble, whatever is right, whatever is pure, whatever is lovely, whatever is admirable—if anything is excellent or praiseworthy—think about such things."*[6] Mike made an acronym to go with this verse, *PLANTREP.* Think on things that are *Pure, Lovely,*

Admirable, Noble, True, Right, Excellent, and *Praiseworthy.* By teaching this to our kids, it reminds us to treat each other better. God takes a step further, and says to think only good things.

He knows that our nature is to speak our minds, and our tongues are often unbridled, especially with our mates. Remember what Mom said, "If you can't say anything nice, don't say anything at all." Quieting the tongue is a lifelong challenge and often requires supernatural discipline. It comes in handy in marriage. When our son was about ten, we were watching a football game, and he said, "The quarterback isn't really cussing, he's just mouthing cusswords." We still laugh about it today.

Sometimes, it's not what we say but the way we look at each other. Coaches use many different hand and body gestures to communicate to their team from the sidelines. These signals can be positive or negative depending on the situation. We need to realize that our body language is always communicating something. Mike says rolling the eyes is contempt. At first, I thought this was a proverb, but I think he just read it somewhere. Wherever it comes from, I have realized it is true. When I roll my eyes, whether I am speaking or not, I am sending a negative message. Even being quiet can get you in trouble if you have a sarcastic look. Our countenance speaks volumes, but our tongues start fires.

How we help each other is demonstrated daily by our consideration of our spouse's needs. Selfless thoughts are less stressful than selfish thoughts. Besides, *God* did not put us here to take care of ourselves or be alone. We were created to be part of something *big*, a team, the Same Team.

The Penalty: Holding, or "You're Keeping Me from Doing What I Want."

The Play: Rick and Diane

When Rick came home from work, he found Heather, the sixteen-year-old from next door, watching the boys. Heather told Rick that his wife, Diane, would be home around six. Diane had told Heather she had to run some errands. Rick had to work through lunch, and he was a little miffed that Diane had not made arrangements for dinner. Diane came bouncing in around six fifteen. She was carrying a few brochures and smiling from ear to ear. Rick asked, "What has you so happy?" Diane announced, "I'm going back to college!" Rick said, "What for?" Diane answered, "You know I always wanted to finish school, and both of the boys are getting older." Rick raised his tone, "School? No dinner tonight, and you haven't even signed up yet? Who's going to take care of the house and the boys? We can't afford Heather every day." Diane bit her tongue and then softly responded, "I only want to take one class, three days a week, to see if I like it." Rick retorted, "Well, I don't like it. One will lead to two, and two will lead to three. Do you want to get a job too? Don't I make enough money?" Diane took a deep breath and said, "Honey, you take care of us just fine. You said last week I should get a hobby. Well, this is my hobby!" Rick gruffed, "I'll have to think about it."

Coach to Rick:

When Rick arrived home to find no wife and no dinner, he could have assumed the best of his wife. He could have made a simple snack or even dinner for him and the boys. This would have moved him from good husband to hero. A hero would *esteem others better than himself.* We should all strive to be her hero. But instead of hero, he felt like it was unfair that he worked so hard, and Diane did not do her job. Then fear crept in—fear that school would interfere with his care and feeding and possibly give him more work around the house. *There is no fear in love, but perfect love casts out fear because fear involves torment.* Rick seemed afraid and acted tormented and agitated. Before Diane came home, Rick knew trouble was brewing inside his heart. That is always a good time to pray for grace and mercy—before the trouble starts.

Husbands, likewise, dwell with them with understanding, giving honor to the wife, as to the weaker vessel, and as being heirs together of the grace of life, that your prayers may not be hindered. Diane going back to school is new and unknown, but Rick should focus on Diane, not himself. *Husbands, love your wives, just as Christ also loved the church and gave Himself for her.* Rick should grab Diane's hand and pray. *The effective, fervent prayer of a righteous man avails much.* We all need to strive to be this righteous man. Diane needs to know that her man looks to God in all decisions and is taking care of both of them. Rick can *trust the LORD with all his heart . . . and He will direct Rick's path.*

Playbook for Rick:

Philippians 2:3, 1 John 4:18, Ephesians 5:25, 1 Peter 3:7, James 5:16, Proverbs 3:5–6

Coach to Diane:

One of the most important aspects of being a woman is that of raising children. These years are just a season in a long, lasting marriage, and they go by quickly. You don't want to miss them. Any mother will tell you they have a full-time job just taking care of the kids. Diane has children that need her, which means her time is not her own. Her husband also has expectations from her, wanting a meal when he comes home. Most men want a special welcome when they get home, whether they say it or not. They would love their wives to greet them at the door and have a meal waiting for them. Coming home to an empty house is not the most comforting experience after a long day at work. When Rick arrives and his wife is not there, things aren't the same as what he's used to.

When Diane arrives, he reacts poorly to what seems to be a simple request.

Diane made the mistake of not asking or consulting him but announcing her new plans. Her going back to school is not a one-sided decision; it affects the entire family. Rick feels disrespected because Diane assumed leadership when she made the decision alone. In marriage, we are to be *like-minded*. How can we choose to go one way without the other supporting us in our path? *Do not be unequally yoked together,* but go down the path together as two, in unison. In football, if the wide receiver runs a different pattern than what was called in the huddle, the quarterback will not be able to complete the pass. The same goes for marriage. A wife is called to be a helper, not a free agent. The team must receive the play in the huddle together. They are led by the coach; this means Diane checks with God in prayer. If God leads her toward school, she asks Rick how he feels about her going back to school. If Rick says he is against it, it means God is against it because we are called to *submit to your husbands as to the Lord,* as God has placed them in a leader-protector role for our benefit. Women are *to be subject to their husbands, so that no one will malign the word of God.*

What is Diane's true motive for wanting to go back to school? Is she feeling devalued now that the boys are getting older? Has she shared her feelings with Rick on why this is important to her? Is she sure it is? Diane needs to take her restless spirit to God and see if this is in His plan for her. If her conversation with Rick goes smoothly and peaceably, she will have her answer. Sometimes when God says no, it means not now. Diane can discern if she and Rick can work out something for her to go back to school in the future, or not, from the peace that she will get *by making her request known to God.*

Playbook for Diane:

Philippians 2:2, 2 Corinthians 6:14, Ephesians 5:22, Titus 2:5, 2 Timothy 2:22, Philippians 4:6

Team Culture—Yours, Mine, and Ours

Failure is not fatal, but failure to change might be.
—John Wooden

Our son is always baffled when players from rival colleges end up playing together on the same team in the NFL. How do they overcome their past differences? How do they go from enemies to teammates? The culture of their former teams has to be replaced with the culture of their new team.

Since 1946, every generation had an identity—Baby Boomers, Generation X, and Generation Y. Within the Boomers, there was the "hippie culture," sometimes called the "counter-culture." They scorned tradition. They did not trust their parents or the "Establishment." Then came the "Me Generation." They were selfish and focused on worldly pleasures. Each generation has their own distinct culture.

Customary beliefs, shared values, attitudes, goals, and practices define a culture. Where do you live? Where are your parents from? How much money do you make? The answers to these questions place you in various subcultures within your generation. Culture is ever changing. Traditions of past cultures change with each new generation. Some of these changes are positive; some are not. Merging two people from different backgrounds creates challenges in marriage.

My home was a combination of Spanish and Italian cultures. Both of my parents were European with the same Catholic upbringing. We spoke English at home, but later it became important to learn Spanish because of the growing Hispanic population in Miami. Both sets of grandparents moved from their countries into a different lifestyle.

At the turn of the century, Europeans arrived at Ellis Island in New York. Many formed subcultures in New York City to maintain their ethnicity—Little Italy, Irish section, Polish section, and Germantown. Wherever you were from, people wanted to be with their own.

Subcultures allowed them to adapt to America with little adjustment. They continued to speak their own languages. They started their own restaurants, groceries, newspapers, and "mom-and-pop" shops.

America became a mixing bowl of cultures over time as we moved from the city into the suburbs. Cities have a few ethnic neighborhoods, but our suburban cultures are defined by how much we make instead of where our ancestors were born. The cultural shifts of the past fifty years have blurred the old lines of tradition. People are getting married with little concern for heritage. The blended result represents several variations in customs.

Today, holiday meals may include many new team influencers such as stepparents, single parents, and live-in partners, bringing different values and ideas to the table. As other cultures and religions come into our homes, old traditions start to fade. When a new marriage merges people from different backgrounds, some families may abandon their religion or adopt a "no religion in the house" attitude to keep things calm. The traditional family of the past has become less common, and single-parent homes are growing at an alarming rate.

According to the U.S. census in 2000, almost one-third of our children live in single-parent households. Most of the societal woes that we face and hear about on the news can be traced to single-parent homes, yet some argue that single parenting is positive. To whom? Possibly this is the justification of single parents who are trying their best to get by. They are forced to create a new normal as a result of a divorce that came from one of the most popular lies: "The kids are better off without hearing their parents argue." The irony is that most of these parents do not understand that a child needs a father and a mother to obtain their identity. Dad provides security to his daughters and identity to his sons. Mom provides identity to her daughters and security to her sons. An overwhelming majority of children will say they want two parents, a mom and a dad, but most parents don't ask the kids before they split up the team.

Some liberal thinkers argue for a religious variety show in the home. They want us to expose our kids to all kinds of false religions and beliefs. They say things like "I want to allow them to decide their own spirituality." These freethinkers don't understand that children need a foundation to understand a belief system. That foundation needs to be established during their early formative years. My husband's divorce created many problems for us in this area. Their mom is Jewish, and we are Christian. Religion became the major difference between Mom and Dad. For the kids, that creates confusion. What they need is consistency. We taught them the backgrounds and similarities of the religion first. We know that Judaism and Christianity are built on the same foundation, which is faith in God and the Bible. So we helped them learn about the Old Testament before exposing them to the New Testament and Jesus. In our house and our church, this is the complete story, and that is what they have chosen to believe. To us, Christianity does not conflict with their Judaism, it completes it. Jesus was Jewish, after all.

We have spent years trying to make the best of a bad situation. We have been blessed by obedience to God's Word, its promises, and His redeeming grace. The undivided team is the winning team. Their focus is in the same direction with the same purpose and vision. Common ground gives you the firm footing you need to deal with the many challenges created by divorce.

Different backgrounds can cause dissention in marriage with fights coming up frequently around holidays, meals, religion, and politics. People from different backgrounds see things differently. Your surroundings influence your decisions. When a quarterback sees a huge tackle coming at him, he may decide to abandon the original play to keep from being crushed. In football, adaptability is part of survival. In marriage, it is important to consider your differences and plan to embrace them. Keep in mind, this cultural background is what formed your "favorite person in the whole wide world."

When you are on the Same Team, it becomes just that—the same. You don't see a basketball player on the gridiron. They don't even use the same ball. They may have similar training schedules and similar interests, but the bottom line is they can't play together. Different rules, different uniforms, different ball. When you mingle cultures and religions, there are many obstacles. We have to know who we are at our core before we can be an effective member of a team. You must know your position. Merging systems are complicated. If it's not important to your identity, you must each be able to give up something from your personal heritage or totally embrace another's for the good of the team.

Can this union ever work? Amazingly, it can if it is built on a strong foundation of a common purpose. We believe Jesus is the anchor for every relationship and especially two sinners from very different backgrounds. The apostle Paul wrote to the Galatians, "There is neither Jew nor Greek, there is neither slave nor free, there is neither male nor female; for you are all one in Christ Jesus."

When the early Jewish followers of Jesus started accepting non-Jewish believers into their church, they first sought to "make them Jewish" through circumcision and dietary laws. Paul explained that this was not necessary due to their like-mindedness and spiritual oneness in belief of Jesus. They later determined that this sameness identified them as one in Christ, and there was no distinction between the Jewish believers and the Greek believers or any other nationality as long as they all had Christ in common. Same Team is founded on the principle in Philippians 2:2, "Being like-minded, having the same love, being of one accord, of one mind."

On a popular TV show, one man gets his choice of twenty-five eligible women to find a wife. It is not a show for children. Sexual lottery is no way to find a mate, but it does provide some interesting insights into the culture of America today and their rationale for finding a partner. I have heard most men say, "I want to make sure I first have an animal attraction and, second, I like to be with her." Women say, "I definitely like to be with him and think he's a nice guy, but I want to make sure we have that physical chemistry." This shows how we approach relationships from two different angles. If we are already starting from different perspectives, we need to find a way to form a true bond.

Many people talk about the physical and emotional connection that they feel for each other but leave out the part that can keep you together for a lifetime—the spiritual bond. This is so important because the other two come from human strength and frailty. The spiritual bond comes from the supernatural and surpasses all knowledge. When you connect your lives together in Christ, you become more than superglue. You become an impenetrable force to be reckoned with through the power of the Holy Spirit. We would love to hear someone say, "I'm going to make sure we're on the same track spiritually before I allow myself emotional or physical attachment."

Why is this spiritual connection so important? If you both believe the same way about God and His Word, you already have a foundation that works. You have a higher power to guide you when your attraction and your bodies fade. When you are sad, tired, weary, disheartened, and bored of each other, He will lift you up. You will not grow weak; you will not fade. You always have a place to go to seek peace and refresh your hearts.

Emotional love is ruled by the heart, and the heart can change. You can't trust your heart. It can get you in trouble. God does not change, and He can be trusted. He is true love, agape love, which is a selfless love that is not physical or emotional. When we surrender our hearts to Him, He will not fail. He is faithful when we are faithless, hopeful in our hopelessness, and loving in our sin. When we are not able, He is able. God's promises to us can bind us against all odds. He transcends the culture of the day. Love will keep us together only if it is God's love. Keeping Christ on our team regardless of our background, outside influences, and the ever-changing culture is the formula for victory.

The Penalty:
Illegal Procedure

The Play: Stan and Karen

Stan has developed a bad habit. He calls his ex-wife to make plans to pick up his kids for the night or the weekend whenever he can without consulting Karen. Stan always takes advantage of any extra time he can spend with his kids, not stopping to consider how this affects Karen's plans or the extra work it gives her.

Karen is a great stepmom and loves the kids as her own, so Stan always assumes that she is ready to take them at a moment's notice. Stan always says, "Any time we can get with the kids is good time." Lately, Stan's business takes him out of town a couple of days a week. Last weekend, the kids were scheduled to be with him, and he had a conference. His ex-wife was accommodating when he asked to switch weekends. He was scheduled to come home on Sunday night. He called Karen on Saturday morning to let her know that he would be home Saturday night instead. Karen was very excited.

After hanging up with him, she began making plans for Saturday night together since they would be alone. She would discuss it with him when he was at the airport. After hanging up with Karen, Stan called his ex-wife to see if he could get the kids on Sunday since he was getting back early. Since the kids live close to the airport, he arranged to pick them up Saturday night on his way home. He expected Karen to be happy about his good news. When he called from the airport to tell Karen that he was bringing the kids home with him, she was extremely disappointed. Karen began whining about the little time they had spent alone over the past two weeks. She also noted how many times she had to drive ninety minutes roundtrip to pick up the kids for various events with no one to help. Stan did not want to have a long-distance argument as he still could not understand why she didn't feel happy about getting them. He was always proud of her relationship with the kids. He said, "I'm going to hang up now. I don't want to have this conversation." Before he could finish his sentence, Karen beat him to it. *Click!*

Coach to Stan:

In Stan's mind, it would be a shame if he ever missed an opportunity to spend time with his children. I am sure Karen feels the same way; however, her husband is making plans with his ex-wife with zero feedback from Karen. This is an episode of doing the right thing the wrong way.

Imagine the coach on the sidelines; he determines the next play in the middle of a critical drive. His All Pro quarterback is waiting in the huddle to receive the play and share it with the rest of the team. One big problem: the coach called the play into his former quarterback who hasn't been on the team for years.

Life is full of complexities. Dealing with a blended family only increases them exponentially. While Stan is working hard to make the best of a bad situation, he is chipping away at his relationship with his favorite person in the whole wide world, Karen. *God* wants us to *be equally yoked, like-minded, of one mind.* Karen, not his ex-wife, is *the one that is going to help him up when he falls, watch his back, and help keep him warm.*

We need to agree on our direction or else we will not be able to journey together. How can Karen be like-minded with Stan if she is kept out of the loop? Yes, the extra phone calls are inconvenient. Yes, many would say they are even inefficient. They are only inefficient if their marriage is less important than time management. Many times, we can use logic and worldly wisdom to argue with God's way, but we are warned that *there is a way that seems right to a man, but in the end, it leads to death.*

Stan was trying to avoid an argument with Karen, but instead, she hung up on him. Could Stan have stayed on the call and hung in there with a different tact? *A gentle response, not a retreat, turns away wrath.* What would be a good gentle response for Stan in this situation? "I'm sorry. I will work harder to understand your feelings."

Playbook for Stan:

Romans 15:5, Philippians 2:2, Deuteronomy 22:10, 2 Corinthians 6:14, Ecclesiastes 4:9–12, Proverbs 14:12, 15:1

Bonus verse—Proverbs 21:1, "The king's heart is like a stream of water directed by the Lord; He guides it wherever He pleases."

Coach to Karen:

Karen has a position with the children and that is "other mother," commonly referred to as stepmom. The word "step" implies not being the first in order of priority. When a couple is in a blended family, it is common for the ex-spouses to communicate frequently regarding the children. That leaves the other spouse out of the loop and can lead to arguments and hurt feelings. No wonder God hates divorce; it creates dual loyalty when children are involved. This plurality of allegiance is a breeding ground for contempt, unless there is excellent communication and understanding between spouses. This is often not the case. The blending of schedules, child support payments, doctor appointments, extracurricular activities, and religious differences all serve to complicate a marriage and create chaos. Karen has to understand that she is an adult and the children didn't ask to be her step kids. Knowing that

Stan wants to see his kids as much as possible, she has to be ready to check his schedule and keep track of visitation to keep her own sanity. Having the kids is an ongoing situation in divorce, and schedules frequently have to be rearranged, especially when one parent works out of town. This means Karen has to use patience and self-control when these changes occur. *Love is patient and kind*, but sometimes we don't naturally feel this way. Karen needs to be mindful of Stan's feelings and his need to connect with his children as often as possible. This will prevent her feeling second to the children or worse, the ex. She must be willing to help him even when it impacts her plans.

Communication is the key in every marriage, and even more in blended families. The lesson of humility is basic in marriage; we must serve one another. Karen must pray to have the same mind as Stan. She can be a powerful example and influence on the children. She is not competing with the past—she has the victory. *"A wise woman builds her home, but a foolish woman tears it down with her own hands."* To build your house, you must be proactive. Karen should check with Stan what he plans upon his return. Understanding avoids disappointment.

We never know when our last moment will be. Make sure we do not leave or hang up with a poor finish. Many have regretted last words said to a loved one in anger. *Put on heartfelt kindness, humility, gentleness, and patience, accepting and forgiving one another, if any has a complaint against the other—just as the Lord has forgiven you.* Above all, Karen has to ask Stan to forgive her for hanging up and put on love, the perfect bond of unity.

Playbook for Karen:

1 Corinthians 13:4, Proverbs 14:1, Colossians 3:12

Communicate? Mama Mia, I'm Italian!

All battles are won before they are fought.

—Sun Tzu

It's late in the game, and the home team needs to get a first down. The quarterback gets the play signaled in from the sidelines. As he enters the huddle, two of the offensive linemen are arguing about who missed their block on the last play. The wide receivers are yelling at the quarterback. Each is arguing that the QB should have thrown them the ball. The running back is trying to yell over everyone else that the play clock is at ten seconds.

Instead of demanding silence in the huddle, the quarterback tries to call the play among the chaos.

We have a chaotic house. I say it is the "loud house." For some reason, we all talk loud. Not like we're screaming at each other, just loud. I always thought it was because of my background—half-Italian and half-Spanish, but then I met my husband. He's even louder than me, and we're not sure what nationality he is because he was adopted. We're pretty sure he's Irish. Ireland must be loud.

If anyone was listening to us, they'd think we were fighting on a daily basis because our voices are boisterous. We are both animated. Our kids are also enthusiastic when they speak. Well, most of them. Our oldest daughter, Madelyn, is mellower when she speaks. When she was younger, I told her if she didn't catch up, we'd steamroll over her because her younger siblings talk 150 miles an hour. Since she took a public speaking class, she has improved greatly. Sometimes she doesn't feel like joining in the competition; this is to her benefit.

With all five of us fighting for air time, communication can get a little intense at our house.

We're improving. Talking over each other creates problems. We need to slow down, listen, and choose our words wisely. Give your brain time to process what your mouth is about to say.

My brother came to visit over the Christmas holidays. We were catching up. He told us that somebody stole his identity over the Internet. Clearing everything up with the banks wasted a lot of time and energy. Before he was finished, I blurted out, "Wait, this is even funnier." My son turned and gave me a look and then looked at my brother and shrugged. "She just says stuff." We ended up laughing about this, but it's just an example of what happens when you're more concerned with what you are going to say than what the other person is saying. We are told to esteem others as more important than ourselves. This is a great communication rule. If we all followed this rule, we'd be a lot better off in our relationships.

Unfortunately, we sometimes hurt each other with our words. We frequently say I'm sorry, but that doesn't make it OK. Family members hurt each other trying to be funny; we say things without thinking how it will affect the other person. Then we realize somebody's not laughing. Good communication is about timing. When we wait for the right time to discuss a matter, we are less apt to fly off the handle or be misunderstood.

On rare occasions, I upset Angel. To avoid confrontation, she may write her thoughts down to share with me later when we are alone. She learned this habit the hard way. Speaking your mind in the moment often leads to hurt feelings that can fuel an argument. When we are angry and out of control, we are not allowing God to work through us. When things start to go sideways, one of us leaves the room to ask God to calm us down and help us choose our words. We work hard to develop this habit. It has allowed situations to correct themselves. Prayer gives us a chance to remember our priorities. It is hard to get upset with a clear head.

Hasty words and actions usually lead to overreaction and end up with someone getting hurt. In a football game, a player can be fined or ejected from the game for an improper verbal reaction. To avoid a penalty, teammates try to remove the angry player from the situation. The Bible tells us, *"Get rid of all bitterness, rage, anger, harsh words, and slander, as well as all types of evil behavior. Instead, be kind to each other, tenderhearted, forgiving one another, just as God through Christ has forgiven you."* [7]

God knows we have a tendency to act out in anger. We must keep ourselves in check. *"Be angry, and do not sin."*[8]

Meditate within your heart and be still. Selah—pause or think it over. The psalmists use this word many times. If we learn how to Selah in marriage, we will create peace in the midst of chaos. The Word says, *"Do not let the sun go down while you are still angry and do not give the devil a foothold."*[9] Many couples married for a long time abide by this and always make up before bedtime. By keeping the devil out of your bedroom, you are fortifying your sanctuary. We remind each other that the devil likes to slip into our house when we are overworked, tired, sick, or anxious. Knowing this, we have to help each other by using kind words and encouragement.

"Do not let any unwholesome talk come out of your mouths, but only what is helpful for building others up according to their needs, that it may benefit those who listen."[10]

When the devil starts to get between you, acknowledge his presence and kick him out. We jokingly say, "Who let the devil in here?" when one of us is overreacting or losing control. The enemy wants to convince us that the argument is personal and that we are against each other. We need to remember that arguments are based on issues and not each other. We are on the Same Team.

Over the years, my words have gotten me into trouble. As a child, I loved attention and spent hours in front of my dad's camera dancing and posing. As an adult, I found that I had no problem speaking in front of people. I actually liked it. Public speaking is the number one fear among adults. That was never my experience. I thought there were plenty of other things to be afraid of like snakes or heights, not talking. When Mike and I met, we were kindred spirits because he wasn't afraid of speaking in public either. We both speak our mind. Neither of us hides our feelings or ideas. This is either wonderful or explosive. Thank goodness, we agree on almost everything when we give each other the chance to completely express our thoughts and opinions.

In one of our couple's Bible studies, we learned about a technique called "five and five." It has been a great help, and it's simple. Each spouse gets to express themselves for five uninterrupted minutes while the other spouse tunes in and listens. When five minutes is up, the other spouse gets their five minutes. It is liberating to express your thoughts and opinions without disruption.

The Bible talks about the damage the tongue can do—how something so small can impact so greatly. James says the tongue is small like the rudder of a boat but can have great impact. The things we say can change the whole course of events. Wars are started by words. *"In the multitude of words sin is not lacking, But he who restrains his lips is wise."*[11] When we talk too much, we are bound to get ourselves into trouble. Why do we feel so compelled to speak? It is because we are allowing ourselves to be controlled by situations, emotions, and others. We think speaking puts us in control, but many times our words remove us from the control position.

"Even a fool is counted wise when he holds his peace; When he shuts his lips, he is considered

perceptive."[12] We can be thought wise simply by shutting up. Easier said than done. No pun intended. In a negotiation, when an offer is on the table, the one who speaks first loses. It is the hardest way to settle a negotiation, but very effective if you are good at it. Unfortunately, most people are not. See what happens the next time you go to buy something and the salesperson talks too much. Some people think the more you talk, the more you will be trusted. Actually, it is the opposite. The person who keeps talking is obviously not listening. How can they understand you and know what you need?

According to an old saying, "No one cares how much you know until they know how much you care." This is human relations 101. When a person is interested in you, they ask questions and then listen to your responses. They want to learn more about you. If you went out on a date and the person spent the entire time talking about themselves, they are either nervous or self-centered. Either way, it's not a good sign. We want to be understood, cared about, and able to communicate our most intimate thoughts to our spouse. We want to build a trusting relationship. When people become overly familiar, they tend to become lazy in their speech. I've heard couples call each other names and swear and curse when they fight. When friends disagree, they hardly ever speak to each other this way. Why do we allow marriage to be grounds for hurling insults to our best friend?

Once you've started this behavior and allowed name-calling or curse words to enter your home, it's hard to stop it from recurring. Name-calling and cursing are out of bounds. You have to set up your boundary lines before you play football. The team can't just run amok all over the field. They stay in the zone. Who's going to blow the whistle in your house when you are out of bounds? Your kids? Your next-door neighbors?

The saying "familiarity breeds contempt" means that you become complacent and sloppy with the people you spend the most time with. You let them see you at your worst. Why not try to be your best every day? Looking your best for each other starts from the inside out. You can keep your inside clean by controlling your negativity and doing positive things for each other. Positive words clean your soul like toothpaste cleans your teeth. Your actions are determined by the way you start your day. Most people don't forget to brush their teeth or comb their hair in the morning. Why do we forget to warm up with God before we face the world?

Every team has a pre-game ritual. It involves warming up and stretching. This prepares them physically. Before they leave the locker room, the coach inspires them and reminds the team of their strengths and their preparedness. This prepares them emotionally.

Begin your day with God. Then when you start to communicate with your spouse, your spirit will be ready. Put on some praise music. Do not allow the TV or the news to be the first influence to affect your attitude. After prayer, try bringing your spouse coffee in the morning or ironing a shirt. Small actions reap great rewards. The first thirty minutes set the tone for your entire day.

When someone knows you are making an effort to care for them, it's harder to start yelling about leaving a towel on the floor or being five minutes late.

If we know it takes supernatural power to control the tongue, why would we try to do it on our own? We can't. It is like a football player expecting to play their best without practice and discipline. How do we become disciplined with our speech when communicating with our spouse? We pray together and for each other. The more we practice, the less we will want to hurt each other with our words. Remember, practice makes permanent (not perfect, think about it). Let your first communication of the day be in prayer, alone or together. The Holy Spirit will take over from there.

I love to write verses with a dry-erase marker on a plate that is on display in my kitchen. All day, as I work, I remind myself what I want to speak into my heart. I change it every month or two depending on what we are going through as a couple, a family, or my own personal struggle. When the kids were out of school and starting to get on each other's nerves, I wrote Philippians 2:14, *"Do everything without complaining or arguing, so that you may become blameless and pure, children of God without fault, in a crooked and depraved generation, in which you shine like stars in the universe."* This verse served as a reminder to stop complaining and arguing and do things that are pure so that we can shine like stars.

We want to be bright lights in a dark world, but we

need to practice being a light to each other at home. We reinforce this is by speaking courteously to each other. Just because we are related doesn't mean we stop saying "please," "thank you," and "excuse me." The more we practice being courteous at home, the less we will fake it in public. It will become part of our character.

Mike still opens my door for me. The children see him modeling that behavior. We want our children to pick partners who will treat them with honor and respect. They need to know what that looks like. If the parents aren't acting respectful, it is hard for kids to comprehend that they must be respectful to adults and each other. We can only expect them to learn what we are willing to model. Teachers do not teach manners class, though there is a definite need. We are teaching our kids by everything we do and say, not only to them but to our spouses and our friends. If they hear you stretch the truth, they will learn to stretch the truth. If they hear you curse, they will curse. Many studies show parents who smoke are more likely to have children who smoke. We are passing down a legacy to our children. Is it positive?

God told the Israelites in Deuteronomy 6, *"These commandments that I give you today are to be upon your hearts. Impress them on your children. Talk about them when you sit at home and when you walk along the road, when you lie down and when you get up."* To teach our children, we have to know these principles and apply them to our own lives as well. Don't just hang them on a wall in your home; talk about them. The more God's Word is active in your life, the more God's promises will begin to come alive. He promises a long life that it may go well for you and your children. Isn't that what we all want? It sounds so easy, yet we fight God by not obeying Him.

If you wanted to be an Olympic athlete and your coach told you to wake up every morning at 5:30 a.m. for stretching, then an hour of running, then weight training for another hour, you wouldn't think that was out of line. You wouldn't argue with the coach. Your only decision is whether or not you want to be an Olympian. You have no guarantee of winning even if you listen and do everything your coach says. God gives us commands and promises to guide us to victory. Husbands and wives have to listen to the Coach to be victorious.

The Penalty: Offsides or "You Talk Before You Listen"

The coach sends in the play from the sidelines. Sometimes the captain on the field makes an adjustment based upon the other team's formation. If a player does not adjust to the captain's audible, there will be confusion. This could lead to a penalty or a big play by the other team. When things are not as they seem, it causes friction and disruption that could cost your team advancement and put you behind. You lose your place after working so hard to get there. If this happens consistently, winning is almost impossible.

The Play: Roger and Sylvia

Roger noticed some water leaking from under the refrigerator. He told Sylvia, his wife, to be careful and he made a call to the dealer because it had only been installed three weeks. Roger was speaking to a very nice clerk from the dealer who said it might not be covered under the manufacturer's warranty. Roger asked why, and when Sylvia heard him, she started telling him that he better get them to fix it—something about their rights, something about an attorney. Meanwhile, the nice clerk said that leaks are often in the water line to the icemaker. The clerk said they would have someone from the dealer out there within two hours to fix it at no charge because the dealer guarantees their installations for twelve months. Roger replied, "OK, thanks," and hung up the phone. Sylvia yelled, "OK, thanks? Way to go, Roger. Once again, you didn't get the job done. Now, I am going to have to call them back and start all over!" With that, Roger flew off the handle and said, "You open your big mouth without knowing what's going on. You have the nerve to disrespect me like I'm some kind of loser, and you have to do everything!" Roger stormed out of the room and went into the backyard to cool off. Just a few minutes later, the refrigerator repairman showed up. After he was finished, Roger and Sylvia still did not speak. Now, it's time for bed and the silent treatment.

Coach to Roger:

This one really looks like it's all Sylvia's fault, but as the leader of the house, Roger has responsibility as well. If we roll back the tape in slow motion, we see Roger committed his own personal foul. He took the defensive position against his wife's offense when he had the ball in the first place. In football, a personal foul is a fifteen-yard penalty, and that's the most you can lose for one penalty. *Your enemy, the devil, is roaming around like a roaring lion looking for someone to devour,* and that someone is you. The "instant spiritual replay" shows the enemy screaming into Sylvia's ear so many slanders against Roger that she could barely hear the phone conversation. Satan only speaks in lies, but sometimes circumstances make us think that our wives are the enemies. Proverbs tell us, *A gentle answer turns away wrath.* The key word is "answer." This means that something was said that could anger or provoke us. The challenging response of an all-pro husband is a gentle one. The apostle Paul tells us that *anger creates a mighty foothold in our home for Satan.* Roger had the opportunity to be *a peacemaker, a son of God.* He could have stayed calm and gently answered, "The repairman will be here within an hour or two at no charge." Then he would have allowed God to address Sylvia's sharp tongue. They both should have withheld their anger as these things happen in houses. It is not anyone's fault. Their frustration at an object turned toward each other, and instead of being slow to anger, they were quick to fly off the handle at the situation. Your anger can never make things right in God's sight. If Roger needed to leave the room to avoid losing control while responding to Sylvia, he should have gone in the backyard to *pray.* To *make his requests known to God so that the peace of God would guard his heart and mind* to quickly forgive and restore them—score!

Playbook for Roger:

1 Peter 5:8, Proverbs 15:1, Ephesians 4:26–7, Matthew 5:8, James 1:19, Philippians 4:6-7

Coach to Sylvia:

Sylvia has clearly shown a lack of respect to Roger and his ability to get things done in the house. This is an attack on his leadership, one of his primary roles as husband. Her quick temper and lack of self-control has turned a small inconvenience about an appliance into "unnecessary roughness." By not having the wisdom to *be slow to speak and quick to listen* to what is really happening, she has missed an opportunity to be thankful to God for putting a nice, helpful clerk on the line with her husband. Being submissive is humbling ourselves to a leader, in this case, our husband. *An excellent wife is a crown to her husband* and *a complaining one is like an incessant dripping* of a faucet. *Love is not irritable and demanding.* Sylvia is criticizing Roger for something that has not even happened or worse for something in the past, in which case, she is *keeping record of his wrongs,* another foul.

Imagine a football game where the referee said, "I think I want to call that penalty from three plays ago, again." The game would never move forward. The same thing happens in marriage when we bring things up from the past. You get stuck back in the old argument instead of dealing with the present situation. *A wise person uses few words and is even-tempered.* We have to control our tongues so that we can give control to the *Holy Spirit who will speak for us in that very hour.* He will tell us if we are to speak or keep silent. Once you start talking, you forget about listening and may jump to conclusions about what's really happening. As wives, we must *stay away from complaining and arguing in everything so that no one can speak a word against us.* It is time for Sylvia to humble herself and reconcile with Roger so that t*he sun does not go down on their anger and give the devil a stronger foothold.* Before we can go to God angry, He tells us to reconcile ourselves with the person who we have fought with and ask forgiveness, even if it's not our fault. Then we should *come boldly to the throne room of grace* for forgiveness from God. As a couple, we are to *serve each other in humility for God sets himself against the proud but shows favor to the humble.*

Though this may seem hard, if she wants to *pursue peace* in her marriage and obtain favor from God, Sylvia must take the first move and advance down the field toward Roger.

Playbook for Sylvia:

James 1:19 NIV, Colossians 3:15, Proverbs 12:4, Proverbs 27:15, 1 Corinthians 13:5, Proverbs 17:27 NLT, James 3:2 NLT, Luke 12:12, Philippians 2:14–15 NLT, Ephesians 4:26-27, Matthew 5:24, Hebrews 4:16, 1 Peter 5:5 NIV, Hebrews 12:14

Clock Management:
Your Time Is Not Your Own

There are 86,400 seconds in a day. It is up to you to decide what to do with them.

—Jim Valvano

Every football wife knows that the longest thirty minutes in her life are the last two minutes of a game.

"Why are they calling a time-out?"

"Why do they keep running the ball in the middle of the field?"

"Why are they punting?"

These questions sound familiar to most husbands that love their wives and football. The last two minutes of a close football game are intense. The fans scrutinize every decision of the coach and the quarterback. How the coach manages the clock throughout the game determines how much time his team actually has for the game-winning drive.

A Google search of songs about time reveals more than fifty pages of lyrics dedicated to this elusive element. Even King Solomon, with all his material possessions, could not own time. In Ecclesiastes, he laments about life's meaninglessness regarding the pursuit of pleasure, wisdom, and work. In chapter three, he acknowledges the inescapable truth of time:

"There is a time for everything, and a season for every activity under heaven:

a time to be born and a time to die,

a time to plant and a time to uproot,

a time to kill and a time to heal,

a time to tear down and a time to build,

a time to weep and a time to laugh,

a time to mourn and a time to dance,

a time to scatter stones and a time to gather them,

a time to embrace and a time to refrain,

a time to search and a time to give up,

a time to keep and a time to throw away,

a time to tear and a time to mend,

a time to be silent and a time to speak,

a time to love and a time to hate,

a time for war and a time for peace."

We have no control over the passage of time. We can choose how we spend our time. In football, clock management is imperative to the outcome of the game. You have four fifteen-minute quarters to play. Your team's performance within the allotted time determines who wins the game. You may have heard the saying, "They just ran out of time." That's not really true. The coach has to make every decision with the clock in mind so when the clock runs out, his team is ahead in points. You can play the best game and still lose if you are not effective at managing the clock.

In marriage, we also need to manage the clock well. We only have 24 hours in a day and 168 hours in a week. In that time, we have to work, take care of our spouse, the kids, the house, the yard, the chores, other family, friends, prayer, study, church. If you have any time left over, you should try to get some rest. Sometimes, it seems like everyone in your life is competing for your minutes.

How do we determine what to do with our time? First, we have to know our true priorities. As Christians, we all know what our priorities are "supposed to be." God is first. Family is second. Work is next. Finally, we are called to serve in our community.

Angel and I have put each other as second only to God. I refer to our kids as "2b." All other family is a distant "2c," relative to my wife and kids. Work comes in third place after God and family. Finally, our church and community gets what is left. That's our family and our priorities. What about yours? You can't manage your life and your marriage around the priorities you should have. If your marriage is out of balance, it is because your schedule doesn't match your priorities.

Try this exercise. Take out a piece of paper for each of you and draw a circle. The circle represents the twenty-four hours in your day. Next, divide your circle into the parts that make up your day. If you work eight hours per day, that is one-third of your chart. If you are one of the lucky few that gets to sleep eight hours, that is another third of your chart. The remaining eight hours will determine whether your clock management is putting your team in a position to win or lose.

Are you committing these precious few hours each day to television, commuting, computer time (e-mail, Facebook, mindless surfing), household chores, or other distractions? Did you include dinner together as a family, time to pray with your kids and as a couple, time to relax and share with your spouse? What about time for intimacy? You look at each other and say, "Our love life should be spontaneous and full of passion." So, how's that working out for you? Are you having sex that should be in the romance novels or do you find yourselves falling on the bed exhausted? Then one of you rolls over and says, "Do you feel like making love?" The other says, "Are you crazy?" That is, if they are still awake at all. Don't worry, we're not laughing either.

This is a serious challenge in marriage. Everything else in our life makes its way onto a schedule or calendar, yet this very important aspect of our marriage goes unscheduled. If it's on your "to-do" list, it is more likely to get done. If it doesn't get scheduled as a priority, it gets put off to tomorrow, the day after, or the day after. Scheduled sex is way better than perfect sex that never happens.

Just like important appointments and meetings, schedule time with each other to plan the future, discuss events, and get to know each other better. This means the kids are not in the room. They may be doing homework, sleeping at home, or at Grandma's. You can be alone in the living room, at the coffee shop, on a walk at the beach or park, or at your favorite restaurant. We read books to each other in bed instead of watching TV. The movies, sporting events, and anyplace else where you are part of an audience is not good for communicating and growing closer to each other. The right setting allows for face-to-face communication without a great deal of noise or interruptions.

Marriage is thousands of days spent with our favorite person in the whole wide world. Do you want to spend those days in battles over what you will do together? Hopefully, you already share common interests that will bond you through the years. Many couples become parents and then empty nesters who have nothing in common. You have to build on common ground, goals, and the things you like to do together. The football players all want to play football. They have a common goal—winning. They plan time to study and practice the plays to achieve their goal. In the same way, we must plan time to be together.

With children, your time is very limited and usually revolves around their activities. Although you may be parents, you are also a husband and wife. Make time to be alone together to remind yourself who you were before and after the children leave. Never stop dating each other. Make your time consistent, whether it's weekly or daily. Don't let time slip away from you as a couple. Many people in counseling say, "We've just grown apart." This doesn't happen overnight. It happens because one spouse has allowed other interests (person, place, or thing) or even the children to overtake their time.

If we don't guard our time together, another person can sneak in between us. You must stay connected to your home team. The players from the Dallas Cowboys don't hang out with the New York Jets. Your home team has to come first in everything you do. If you can't find the time, make the time. Spend the time with your team, or you may end up losing the game. Use your clock wisely, and at the end of the fourth quarter, your team is a winner.

Penalty: Illegal Shift

It is a constant struggle to be aware of your schedule and coordinate with your spouse, but winning teams make it a priority. When they are in rhythm, the quarterback knows where his receivers are before he throws. Likewise, the receiver expects the ball to be there when he turns around. The members of the Same Team strive to stay in sync.

The Play: Frank and Iris

Over the past ten years, Frank's job has involved traveling around the country two to three days a week. Frank usually knows where he is traveling two weeks ahead of time, but he always seems to make the arrangements at the last minute. Iris is left juggling her schedule to meet the family's needs and maintain stability for the children. This creates stress as she likes to have dinner, kid's activities, and her own appointments coordinated with Frank's trips so she can be available for him. This time Frank needs to be in Wisconsin for an early morning meeting. There are no direct flights from Florida. This means Frank will fly in the night before; so he chose the latest possible flight. This gives him time to have dinner with his family. Frank told Iris he was leaving Wednesday night, but he was vague about the time. Iris's friend, Nancy, called to make plans for Wednesday night. Iris jumped at the opportunity because she knew Frank would be leaving, and it would not take time from being with him. On Wednesday night, Frank was spending time with Iris when Nancy showed up at the door. Iris reminded Frank that she and Nancy were going to dinner. Frank arranged his schedule so he could spend extra time with Iris. When she left forty-five minutes before him, he was upset. He decided to let it go for now. He would bring it up next time she complained about his traveling.

Coach to Frank:

The good news is that after ten years of marriage, Frank is starting to get a clue, but not quite yet. He went out of his way to allow for extra time with his wife prior to this trip. This was great progress in his mind. Iris would have shared his victory if she only knew the details. Frank's last-minute planning and vague details are comparable to a quarterback drawing a few lines in the dirt and then calling out the ultimate play, "Just get open." This play usually meets with the same fate as Frank's poorly defined plan. Frank is successful at work because he can see ahead and make clear plans to move forward. He can devise action plans to achieve targets and objectives and make high-level decisions. At home, he needs to work on sharing his plays with Iris so she can work with him and help him.

Plans go wrong for lack of advice. Instead, Frank feels like Iris is working against him. Frank is called to *be like-minded, having the same love, being of one accord, of one mind.* If he is honest with himself, he knows that Iris would have never left early if she knew Frank was leaving later. Although he is disappointed, Frank must *guard his heart* and mind against *anger because anger gives a mighty foothold to the devil.* We never want to give Satan a chance to dig in against the team.

Playbook for Frank:

Proverbs 15:22 NLT, Philippians 2:2, Proverbs 4:23 NLT, Ephesians 4:27 NLT

Coach to Iris:

Iris knows that if she wants to know Frank's itinerary, she needs to check with him by asking and not setting him up to fail. If Iris commits to incorporate Frank's travel itineraries into her day timer, she will know the details and minimize future miscommunications. Frank is considerate about making as much time as possible to be with her by waiting until the last minute to leave on business trips. When Nancy called, Iris thought it was perfect timing for two friends to get together the same night Frank was leaving. She assumed she wouldn't miss any time away from him by going out with her friend. One of the ground rules Frank and Iris set up for their marriage is "time together wins over time with friends." When she saw Frank's facial expression as she was leaving, she knew trouble was brewing even though he didn't mention it. She could hardly have a good time visiting with Nancy when she kept thinking that she had let Frank down without really doing anything wrong. She knows God would not want her to be anxious, *but give all your worries and cares to God*. She should pray that God would change Frank's heart and *not have him bitter or angry toward her*. Iris should not go to sleep without calling Frank to apologize for the miscommunication, regardless of who is right. *She may win Frank over by her conduct*. Iris knows that when her man feels slighted, there is no time for hesitation. *Now is the time to forgive and comfort him*. If *she can be trusted with very little* like this, God will bless her when bigger issues present themselves.

Playbook for Iris:

1 Peter 5:7 NLT, Ephesians 4:31 NLT, 1 Peter 3:1, 2 Corinthians 2:7 NLT, Luke 16:10 NIV

What's Yours Is Mine and Mine Is Whose?

Ordinary riches can be stolen; real riches cannot.
In your soul are infinitely precious things that
cannot be taken from you.

—Oscar Wilde

A couple came into the office for premarital counseling. The bride was older, and she brought a considerable financial advantage into the marriage. The husband-to-be owned a house but barely made enough to take care of himself. They thought they would be able to live cheaper together, but the wife wasn't ready to give up her assets or comingle their funds. How would you describe the foundation for this marriage?

Some people want to get a prenuptial agreement to protect themselves financially "just in case." This means, "I don't fully trust you yet, so I am not ready to share my treasures with you, but I will share the house, the bed, and maybe a kid or two." Money seems to be more important than the intimacy of our bodies. It is better to build your trust over time than to rush in and hope it will come later.

Angel asked me to sign a prenuptial agreement. She was concerned because she was burned financially in her previous marriage. She asked her dad, and he agreed it would be prudent. I told her I would pray about it. After much prayer, I refused to sign the agreement because it introduced the idea of divorce even before our wedding day. Angel agreed but was worried her dad might get upset with our decision. We knew we could not start our marriage on a foundation of "just in case." When she told him there would be no prenup, her father amazingly had no issue whatsoever. The unanimous decision confirmed the Lord had directed our steps.

This problem is common in households where one of the partners has suffered financial loss due to a prior divorce. Money is still the number one cause of marital discord and brings more couples to counseling and eventually divorce court than any other issue. Ironically, most people are worse off financially after divorce than while they were married.

Money has emotional ties. We have been taught that money can give us things that make us happy. This lie has led many down a path of crime, drugs, alcohol, gambling, and ultimate destruction. Money does not buy happiness. Solomon was the richest king of all time. He had everything money could buy, yet he expressed in Ecclesiastes, "Life is meaningless." After a life filled with riches, he knew that without God, even the "good life" was a dead end.

Look at the magazine covers in the grocery store line. They show one celebrity after another, even with all their millions, having problems with addiction, infidelity, weight control, and child custody battles. Look at the rock stars and actors who have committed suicide. It seems that they had it all. If your "all" is defined by money, you will never have enough. Jesus taught us not to seek after things that do not last.

"Do not lay up for yourselves treasures on earth, where moth and rust destroy and where thieves break in and steal; but lay up for yourselves treasures in

heaven, where neither moth nor rust destroys and where thieves do not break in and steal. For where your treasure is, there your heart will be also." [13]

He knew we could sell our souls for material possessions that will not satisfy.

Our attitude about money, how we spend it, save it, control others with it, and give it away impacts our team on a daily basis. On a football team, one player may be compensated more than another. This may seem unfair, but this is how the world runs. One employee receives a higher salary than the other employee. The brick layer doesn't make as much as the land developer. The doctor may not make as much as the attorney he hires. Money is a form of reward, but it is distributed differently depending on skill level and where you live. The cost of living in New York is much higher than Iowa. It is hard to understand the fairness of money; some have a lot and some have little.

What do you do with what you are given? The parable of the talents gives us a good illustration of how we can use money.

"Again, it will be like a man going on a journey, who called his servants and entrusted his property to

them. To one he gave five talents of money, to another two talents, and to another one talent, each according to his ability. Then he went on his journey. The man who had received the five talents went at once and put his money to work and gained five more. So also, the one with the two talents gained two more. But the man who had received the one talent went off, dug a hole in the ground and hid his master's money.

After a long time the master of those servants returned and settled accounts with them. The man who had received the five talents brought the other five. 'Master,' he said, 'you entrusted me with five talents. See, I have gained five more.'

His master replied, 'Well done, good and faithful servant! You have been faithful with a few things; I will put you in charge of many things. Come and share your master's happiness!' " [14]

This teaches us that no matter how much we start with, our decisions dictate what we will have in the future. God can choose to give us more if we are good and faithful with what we have. Poor money management has negative consequences.

"But the master replied, 'You wicked and lazy servant! If you knew I harvested crops I didn't plant and gathered crops I didn't cultivate, why didn't you deposit my money in the bank? At least I could have gotten some interest on it.'

Then he ordered, 'Take the money from this servant, and give it to the one with the ten bags of silver. To those who use well what they are given, even more will be given, and they will have an abundance. But from those who do nothing, even what little they have will be taken away.'" [15]

Sometimes fear will keep us from making good decisions with our money, and we lose the little we had to begin with. Laziness can also make us lose our money. The Bible says, *"If anyone will not work, neither shall he eat."*[16] That's easy to understand.

When we get married, we know there will be "work for food" like the sign says. Who does what? How will we spend what we get? This could feed an argument. When the husband maintains his role as provider, the wife feels more secure.

Wives, if you believe your husband is not providing enough for your house, what do you do?

A. Get a job to make up for his shortfall.

B. Inspire him to make more.

C. Nag and complain to remind him of what a failure he is.

D. Analyze your household spending to see if there are ways you can live on less.

Although there is no perfect answer, there are definitely wrong answers. Nagging and complaining are not helpful. Same Team is about knowing your position on the team and following the coach's instructions. There may be a time for the wife to work or a time to cut back. By seeking God's will for your marriage, you will be in alignment on these issues. It is always the role of the wife to inspire her husband to be his best.

If a man cannot lead, provide, and protect, his wife may be reluctant to trust him. Some wives seek to fulfill those roles themselves. The wife becomes executive, mother, father, and superwoman. These sad trends are leading to a fatherless generation. Husbands have to fulfill their roles and lean on God to deliver. *"But if anyone does not provide for his own, and especially for those of his household, he has denied the faith and is worse than an unbeliever."*[17]

Every team experiences tough times. God teaches us most of our lessons through trials. Divine lessons do not indicate sin or weakness. They represent God's enduring love for each of us. He yearns to have our hearts open to his will. We learn to draw closer to God as we struggle.

Professional football players don't appear to struggle financially. They enjoy a lifestyle provided by their efforts. They play for a trophy, which none of them get to keep, and a flamboyant ring they rarely wear. The few players that win the Super Bowl receive fame and fortune, but they will be left asking themselves, "What's next?"

Husbands and wives succeed by keeping a heavenly focus. Our greatest treasures await us in eternity. Our marriage is more important than the size of our house, the make of our car, or our career accomplishments. Money is important as a tool. We have to learn to master it. We cannot allow money to rule over us. Jesus talked about money more than any other topic. He understood our hearts and the power of money. When we make money our treasure, we miss all the simple pleasures that God wants to share with us. Sharing money with your spouse can be fun if you agree, trust God, and master money together.

Who Keeps the Books?

One of the first questions in a new marriage is "Who will pay the bills?" The spouse that maintains the checkbook does not necessarily make the most money. When one of you is gifted in this area, we recommend that person keeps the records. If both of you are good with tracking income and expenses, you should determine which one has time to do it. Setting up a home means combining funds. Marriage is usually the first time you will experience sharing money with someone. Companies have accountants to keep control over the spending and savings of their firm. A marriage needs a similar system of accountability.

You should both be aware of the records, what's in them and where they are kept. You both need to know the passwords. Giving your checkbook over to someone takes a high degree of trust. Knowing how your partner maintained their finances before you married is a good indicator of their record keeping in the future. Finding out later that they never balanced their checkbook or have not paid their bills can be disastrous on the relationship. When you become one, you also become one credit score for all future purchases. This fact alone can hinder a couple from achieving their goals for years.

Your team needs to have discussions on how you spend and save money, what you spend it on, when you spend it, and how you make those decisions as a couple. We recommend setting a standard amount that you both agree you can spend without checking with the other person. Whether this is $50 or $500 is not important, the agreement in advance will avoid grief later. This boundary helps overcome the temptation of a sale and the power of a coupon. Whether I'm in the hardware store or Angel is at the department store, we seem to find unbelievable deals that we can't pass up. If it is within our agreed-upon boundary, we buy it if it makes sense. If it is more than we agreed, we call each other to discuss the purchase. We ask each other a powerful question, "Is this a life changer?"

Angel and I went to the Home Show. Living in South Florida, fireplaces are rare, but a fireplace was on our wish list. We found a fake fireplace that used fuel cans to provide real fire. We agreed it would be a life changer. We put it in our living room. Previously, we never sat in the living room. Since we bought our fireplace, we start every morning in our living room praying and reading. We hold all family meetings in the living room. The fireplace became the centerpiece of our family and a true life changer.

Give It Away

"Charity begins at home" has its origins from the Bible. We are told to *"share your food with the hungry and to provide the poor wanderer with shelter—when you see the naked, to clothe him, and not to turn away from your own flesh and blood."* [18]

Along with our families, our community is our responsibility. God talks about the tithe and its purpose. It's about faith, not about God needing our money. The tithe started as a free will offering given by the Israelites to the priests to maintain their place of worship. When we give to the church, it is not about constructing a building but providing for and building up the body of Christ.

Newlyweds are excited to start their new home. Every strong house is built on a firm foundation. In God's economy, 90 percent of everything we earn is for our house, and 10 percent is for His house. The tenth that you give to His house actually strengthens your house. If you struggle as a couple to give, you will find struggle in your life.

Remember this: *"Whoever sows sparingly will also reap sparingly, and whoever sows generously will also reap generously. Each of you should give what you have decided in your heart to give, not reluctantly or under compulsion, for God loves a cheerful giver. And God is able to bless you abundantly, so that in all things at all times, having all that you need, you will abound in every good work."*[19]

How does a couple know how to tithe? It sounds easy, right? Pay all your bills and magically, you're left with 10 percent. If you have ever tried this, you know this doesn't work. Our Head Coach uses tithing to strengthen our faith muscles. By giving our tithe first, we have to rely on Him to cover the rest of our bills. God knows our hearts and our tendency to want to keep everything for ourselves. The more we experience giving, the easier it becomes. People that come into marriage with different views on giving will find a constant battle going on in their home.

By studying God's Word and testing Him, He will reveal His truth to you. Are we allowed to test God? *"Bring the whole tithe into the storehouse, that there may be food in my house. Test me in this," says the LORD Almighty, "and see if I will not throw open the floodgates of heaven and pour out so much blessing that you will not have room enough for it."* [20]

The first time I read this, I was struggling with tithing. As a new believer and newly married with three stepchildren, I couldn't see how we could give this kind of money and still pay child support. One day, I heard a story on the radio that began to change my heart. A lady wanted to give to her church, but her husband forbade her to tithe. She asked him if she could give a smaller amount with the condition that if they were worse off the next year, she would not continue to give that much. Her husband agreed. Of course, the next year they had more.

My husband was telling me to give more, but being the bookkeeper at home, I could not see where we could afford it. I shared this with a friend of mine, and she explained to me a tithing method that really works. She told me to write the tithe check first. I was skeptical, but after several arguments, my husband said I could give any amount I wanted. He agreed because he was told by an elder that God did not want us fighting over tithing.

In the first year, I tested God with a 3 percent offering. I am ashamed to say it took several years of testing. I now tithe with a cheerful heart as I have witnessed God's blessing on our family year after year. Our minivan episode was a breakthrough in my faith.

We were in the middle of negotiating for a new car. Our research showed our van was worth $8,000 as a trade. The dealer offered a much smaller amount. I said to myself, "I would rather give it away." I thought aloud, "Maybe we should donate it." Mike suggested I call Sheridan House, a local ministry, right away (in fear of me changing my mind). Reluctantly, I called them. One of their ministries supports single moms.

"If I was to donate my minivan, how would that work?"

Before explaining the details, the receptionist said, "A minivan! That would be so awesome!"

"Why?"

"This morning, a request came from a single mom with three toddlers—all in car seats. She desperately needs a vehicle, and only a minivan could handle all the car seats."

GOD confirmed it. Our title was transferred by lunch. They gave us a donation receipt for $8,000. It's never about the money. It is God teaching us that we can trust Him.

We shared the story and the lesson with our kids. Our kids named all our cars. This one was Big Blue. The Sheridan House newsletter came the next month with a picture of a single mom with her three toddlers in Big Blue. We were all inspired.

The lesson continued the following year. When we prepared our tax return, the IRS owed us a refund. The refund amount was $8,000. As I opened the check from the IRS, I thought I heard God laughing.

The Penalty: Running the Wrong Play, or "You Went Ou of Our Agreement"

This is the equivalent of an incomplete pass. We have all seen the frustration of a quarterback that throws a pass to a spot that he and the receiver had both agreed upon, and the receiver is not there. The enemy is there to intercept at those times and put your team on the defense.

The Play: Bob and Susie

Bob and Susie had agreed as a couple that each of them could spend up to $200 on a new purchase if they were ever shopping without the other. If the item ran over $200, they would have to discuss it before buying. On a business trip, Bob's colleague, Jim, just received a new set of the latest golf clubs. Jim said he would give Bob a great deal on his old set, (six-month-old

Titaniums), but he had to know right away because Jim's brother-in-law would buy them if Bob didn't. His brother-in-law was coming in tomorrow and Jim had both sets with him. Bob tried to reach Susie on her cell phone and at home, but she wasn't answering either one. Susie couldn't answer because she was giving one of the kids a bath and later forgot to check her messages. That night, Bob walked into the house excitedly announcing to Susie that he got an unbelievable deal on a six-month-old set of Titaniums for only $350. "They're worth a grand!" Bob exclaimed. Susie's face fell, and her disappointment was apparent in her body language. She slumped down on the couch and slapped her hands on her knees. Bob's excitement turned to anger and an argument ensued.

Coach to Bob:

Before we discuss how right Bob was in getting a great deal on an awesome set of clubs, we have to ask ourselves a few questions. Is this argument about money? Does it matter whether or not they can afford it? As leader of the home, does Quarterback Bob have the authority to call an audible? Anybody at work would tell you that Bob is a man of his word. Is he a man of his word at home? As a man, it is easy to find twenty different reasons to justify the purchase. As a man of God, there is a different view. Was Bob eyeing (coveting) Jim's clubs prior to this "deal"? After Bob couldn't reach Susie, he just couldn't pass up this "once-in-a-lifetime" opportunity. There is no such thing in God's provision as a "once-in-a-lifetime" opportunity.

Bob should *put on the Lord Jesus Christ and make no provision for the flesh, to fulfill its lusts.* Then he should pray about the decision. To finish the play well, Bob would call Susie again, even though she might not have agreed. In the back of his mind, he was hoping she wasn't home. If God wanted Bob to have these clubs, he would have provided them in a way that would not cause him to break his agreement with Susie. No matter how tempting the deal, *God is faithful. He will keep his temptations* of *buying golf clubs from becoming so strong that* Bob *can't stand up to it.* God will provide a solution that does not involve Bob breaking his promise with Susie. Bob needs to *trust God and His faithfulness because He will show him a way.* Bob's excessive desire or greed clouded his judgment. *Greed causes fighting; trusting the Lord leads to prosperity.* If God wants Bob to have golf clubs, they will come with *peace that surpasses all understanding.*

Playbook for Bob:

Romans 13:14, 1 Corinthians 10:13 NLT, Proverbs 28:25 NLT, Philippians 4:7

Coach to Susie:

Susie could have avoided this argument by using a *gentle answer* as her first response, which *turns away wrath*. This is a tough assignment for her because Bob has not acknowledged any wrongdoing. Her anger over the broken agreement regarding expenditures is really not about money as much as about trust, loyalty, and commitment—all key ingredients in marriage. Susie has to *guard her heart* against reacting and put herself in Bob's shoes. She could have easily fallen into similar temptation had it been a new tennis racquet or a stunning pair of shoes. How would she have felt if she had done the exact same thing? *If Susie claims to be religious but doesn't control her tongue, she is fooling herself, and her religion is worthless.* She needs to control her tongue so she has no regret later. *Love is not irritable.*

So if she really wants to talk to him about how this made her feel, it is in her best interest to n*ot allow the devil a foothold* by allowing her anger to control her. She must know that *anger can never make things right with God.* The devil comes in by tempting Susie to fall prey to sin by using her actions to prevent her from forgiving Bob. Susie must walk away and pray that the Holy Spirit will rule her and settle in her heart that *now is the time to forgive him and comfort him; otherwise he may become so discouraged that he won't be able to recover.* She must show him that in spite of his decision, she still loves and respects his ability to make wise decisions, but she wants them to *be like-minded* in the spending department and *in all things.* It is important for her to first respect Bob and listen to his rationale before flying off the handle. Next time she wants to explain her feelings and desires for their relationship, Bob is more likely to listen. There are no independent winners or losers in marriage. You can both be losers or choose to be winners together when you're on the Same Team!

Playbook for Susie:

Proverbs 15:1 NIV, Philippians 4:7, James 1:26 NLT, 1 Corinthians 13:5 NLT, Ephesians 4:27 NLT, James 1:19–20, 2 Corinthians 2:7 NLT, Philippians 2:2

Sex: First and Ten, Let's Do It Again!

When there is nothing to lose by trying and a great deal to gain if successful, by all means, try.
—W. Clement Stone

The whistle blows. Everyone is exhausted. The coach ran the team hard all day. He needs his team to be in shape for the first game that is less than a week away. He calls everyone on the team around him to wrap up the practice. He starts, "A rookie came in first on every sprint we ran today. If I was a veteran, I wouldn't feel good about losing to a rookie—every time. Tomorrow's a new day, and I better see a new attitude in my veterans."

Coaches love rookies. They have high energy, and they will do anything to impress the coach. The coach can use the passion of the rookies to motivate the veterans. A coach can build a team around a few veterans that do everything with the zeal of a rookie. Why do some veterans lose their enthusiasm to practice and compete? They get comfortable. They get tired. They get bad ideas from themselves and outside influences. Team dynamics change. The goal is to stay motivated and energized throughout their career.

We attended a Hispanic wedding. Mike had to wear a translator so he could understand the ceremony, which was performed in Spanish. The pastor looked at the bride and said, "One of the things you must remember to have a successful marriage is to have sex as often as possible, even if you don't want to, and even when he doesn't ask for it." Everyone chuckled, and many of the women looked at each other and giggled or rolled their eyes, depending on their marital status. Mike said the woman translator stopped translating to ask her colleague, "Did he just say that?" I have been married long enough to know the pastor was right. I did not have this understanding when I was first married. I wish I did.

The priority and frequency of sex in marriage is

usually not the same for both partners. Women's needs change with their hormonal cycle. They also have to deal with what is happening at work, the children, and the amount of time left at the end of a busy day. As a result, sex can fall off the schedule. Men are more consistent with sex—they want it all the time, tired or not, kids or no kids. It's no surprise that the all-Spanish wedding ceremony is Mike's favorite.

Something that is supposed to be pleasurable can bring stress into the relationship when both partners are not in sync sexually. Most married couples have issues with frequency, quality, the time, and the place that sex fits into their routine. Issues of boredom or constant tiredness are warning signs that the marriage needs its batteries recharged. Both spouses have to work to keep their sexual desire for each other from fading.

Marriage is not an excuse to let yourself go. It can be a sad day when you look back on your wedding pictures and wonder where those two people went. A wedding ring is not a license to give up trying to please each other physically and relationally. We have to work hard to look great and act great toward each other.

In football, players make mistakes due to familiarity. They miss practice or ignore the game films. They fall into the rut of "same ol' same ol'." Learning new plays and staying in shape will keep them playing well for years. In marriage, staying physically fit also helps with sex. We need to keep "woo" in our relationship to keep things interesting. Woo means to seek the favor, affection, or love of another. Your "home team" should be in a constant state of woo.

There are several ways to stay in woo. We want to inspire you to stay in tune physically with each other. The Song of Solomon is a lover's guide in the middle of the Bible. If you want to get in the mood, read this together. Husbands read the lines of "The Beloved," and wives read the lines of "The Shulamite."

Getting in the mood is critical for good sex— celebrating the oneness of your marriage. Angel thinks I am always in the mood. This is mostly true, but she requires some warm-up time. Every football team goes through warm-ups before the game. It is a time of transition. Most of the time, we were doing household chores within an hour of making love. If you want her to enjoy making love more than she enjoyed making dinner, you have go through warm-ups. On every team, some players need more time to warm up than others. Players that warm up the best perform the best.

God wants husbands and wives to be sexually fulfilled. That is why he blesses the marriage bed. *"Marriage is honorable among all, and the bed undefiled . . ."*[21] God wants us to have sex with only our spouse, and the marriage will be honored because of our purity to each other. Sex is good. Sex is biblical. Sex is reserved for married people. As men, we are to keep our bodies for our wives, and wives keep your bodies for your husbands. Paul explains:

"The wife does not have authority over her own body, but the husband does. And likewise the husband does not have authority over his own body, but the wife does."[22]

Many people don't know these verses are in the Bible. Our bodies belong to our spouses. We are supposed to take care of them for their sakes. Care includes external and internal. We need to present our best for our favorite person in the whole wide world. Sloppy dress and looking unkempt reflects poorly on us, and it is a poor representation of our spouse and family. How you look on the outside affects how you feel on the inside. Are you taking care of your health? This includes what you eat, the vitamins and supplements you take, exercise, and regular checkups. Some of us do more preventive maintenance on our cars than we do on our bodies.

A professional football player does not show up to the stadium five minutes before kickoff. He shows up several hours before the game to prepare. He stretches. He runs some plays. He gets mentally prepared for the other team. How much do we prepare for sex? Little effort and poor preparation will lead to hurried sex or no sex. Although spontaneity may seem romantic, reality may dictate a scheduled time for sex. We schedule everything else that is important. Sex is important.

Paul continues to the Corinthians:

"Do not deprive each other except by mutual consent and for a time, so that you may devote yourselves to prayer. Then come together again so that Satan will not tempt you because of your lack of self-control." [23]

Paul warns us not to hold back sexually from each other unless you have both agreed to "fast from sex" for a period of special prayer time. Withholding sex for any other reason is a sin. You are helping Satan tempt you and your spouse. This is playing with fire. Unanswered sexual advances lead to feelings of frustration and anger. If sex is neglected for too long, it may lead to adultery, pornography, or nonsexual destructive behaviors such as overeating.

"I'm not in the mood" can mean "I don't feel good," "I'm tired," or "I'm still remembering something you said earlier today." The man hears this and feels rejected not realizing his wife is harboring ill feelings that have zapped her enthusiasm. Keep in touch during the day so you will be connected at night. Set up "together time" throughout the day. This starts with prayer together, breakfast, and a good morning kiss. Then check in on each other in the middle of the day. This keeps your schedules aligned, and it is a great opportunity for encouragement and kind words. Then be ready to greet each other with open arms and open ears at the end of the day.

If TV is stealing two to three hours every night, you need to reprioritize your time. Television does not bond you together. It separates your eye contact and inhibits healthy communication. Stop television from robbing your marriage.

You will be surprised and pleased with the extra time and energy you gain by taking back this precious connecting time. Keep sex alive by looking your best, feeling your best, and making time for each other through every season. Sex in marriage is a required fundamental, both physically and spiritually. Put your next "home game" on the schedule and don't let anything rain it out. Just do it.

The Penalty: "Audible" Disagreement

The quarterback comes up under center. As he is barking out code that only his team understands, he notices that the linebacker has shifted to the left. If they run the play that he called in the huddle, that linebacker will be in position for an easy interception. He adds additional codes as he yells out what seems to be random letters, numbers, and colors. To his teammates, it is a new set of instructions. Football can be very complex. The players have to deal with the enemy, decipher code, and adapt to new plays—all in less than ten seconds. The quarterback calls an "audible," a change in the play to adapt to the enemy's attack. If someone on the team does not change their actions according to the "audible," the results are often disastrous.

The Play: Janey and Todd

Janey had quite a day. First thing, she locked her keys in the car in the front yard and had to wait forty-five minutes for the emergency assistance to come. Then her boss was standing right in front of her office when she showed up late. To top it off, sales results are down for the week and the manager's meeting went until 6:30 pm. By the time she got home and changed into gym clothes, she was too tired to go. Looking in the refrigerator she saw two cans of tuna and whipped up a casserole for Todd. He walked in the door at 7:15 pm and said, "What's for dinner?" Janey barked back, "Tuna casserole and if you don't like it, too bad. I've had a tough day and just got home myself." After dinner, Todd was rubbing Janey's leg on the couch and she knew that meant he would be wanting to go to bed early and get romantic. Janey said, "I hope you're not expecting sex tonight. I'm exhausted and just want to 'veg' out." Todd looked hurt and then spouted, "You're always tired or have a headache. I work hard too, but I don't turn our time together into a chore like you do. When are you going to learn to relax and think about me for a change?" Janey went off, "You, you, you! Why can't I just have some private time when I come home instead of catering to you? It's all about you!" At that point, Todd got up from the couch and left the room. Janey was glad that she could watch her TV show in silence. When she finally came to bed, Todd was snoring loudly. She thought to herself, "Oh well, at least I can go to sleep now if I can keep him quiet." The next morning, Todd told Janey he wouldn't be home until late because he was meeting some guys to watch the game. Janey started to wonder if she was pushing him away.

Coach to Todd:

At seven fifteen, Todd ran into a cornerback blitz. Todd was able to avoid a loss on the play by not responding angrily. *A harsh word stirs up anger.* Janey appears to have her entire day's problems bottled up to unleash on Todd. Did Todd go the whole day without checking in with Janey? Todd needs to *be diligent to know the state of his flocks.* A quarterback is like a good shepherd; he does whatever is necessary to help the team/flock to be its best. This practice allows Todd and Janey to help each other throughout the day. *Two are better than one, for if they fall, one will lift up his companion. But woe to Janey who is alone when she falls, for she has no one to help her up. Though Todd may be overpowered by another,* Todd and Janey *can withstand him.*

When Janey barked, Todd had an opportunity to be a hero. An ordinary play could have become a game breaker. For Todd, it would have been a tough play after a hard day's work, but it's the extra effort that makes an all pro. After Todd avoided the early blitz, he should have thrown up a prayer, asking for God's help and wisdom in a difficult situation. God's grace and humility would guide Todd to help Janey address her needs before his own. Todd shouldn't be *selfish* . . . he needs to be *humble, thinking of Janey as better than himself.* In order to accomplish this, we need to practice listening, massages, dishwashing, and making her day finish well. These are foreign to most of us. At first, these drills will create a strange feeling in your stomach. They are definitely tough, but with practice, you will learn to master them and your team will be stronger for it.

One of the most common offenses the devil uses against marriage is the sexual advance. We see it when Todd goes for the close by rubbing Janey's leg. The devil says, "If she loves you, she will want to have sex whenever you do (just like on TV)." We need to remember that our wives do love us. They may be mad—at us or something else—but they love us. If Todd leads by example, he will take care of Janey. She will follow his example and eventually take care of him. God calls us to be patient and humble.

Todd totally fumbles the ball when he goes to bed angry. This is a personal foul, fifteen yards. Todd should *not let the sun go down on his wrath.* Todd's *anger gives the devil a foothold* in his house. It's like having the enemy in your huddle. We see the results the next morning when he announces that he is going to be playing with another team tonight because he is not happy with the home team. In an attempt to repay her for last night's cold shoulder, he pulls a punk play that the enemy will use to attack both him and Janey. Our playbook clearly says, *"Love keeps no record of wrongs."* Todd better review the playbook before the game gets out of hand. *All Scripture is inspired by God and is useful to teach us what is true and to make us realize what is wrong in our lives. It corrects us when we are wrong and teaches us to do what is right.*

Playbook for Todd:

Proverbs 15:1, Proverbs 27:23, Ecclesiastes 4:10–12, Philippians 2:3 NLT, Ephesians 4:26–27 NIV, 1 Corinthians 13:5 NIV, 2 Timothy 3:16 NLT

Coach to Janey:

Love is patient, love is kind. It is not rude, it is not self-seeking, it is not easily angered, it keeps no record of wrongs. Does Janey remember this part of her vows? She is allowing outside pressures to rule her relationship with Todd, who has done nothing wrong or out of the ordinary. She is taking her "bad day" out on him. She probably wouldn't treat a friend or her mother this way, but Todd gets a dose of her wrath just for coming home. And we wonder why some guys want to go out for drinks after work. If this is what was waiting for you, would you want to go home? *A gentle answer turns away wrath, but a harsh word stirs up anger.* How Janey speaks to Todd will affect how Todd reacts. Her communication can be well received and understood, or ill received and misunderstood—even worse, ignored. Janey did not have to add quarrelsome words in her answer to Todd regarding the dinner. *It's better to live alone in the desert than with a*

quarrelsome, complaining wife. Is Janey really trying to send Todd to the desert by her actions? Hurting words usually lead to hurtful actions, and now Janey is withholding affection and sex from her husband. This is a definite penalty for the Same Team. Janey should not deprive Todd of sex without a real reason. Janey has come home angry and Todd is in her sights. She needs to understand that marriage is about two people's lives, not her day versus his day. Sex is supposed to draw us closer in our marriage and not to be used as a weapon against each other when we are angry. There will be times when you're not in the mood, but God will bless your effort to encourage your mate sexually. Just as Janey wants her needs met, Todd wants his needs met in another way. Janey will be blessed for humbling herself to him, especially when she doesn't want to. The only fast we should have from *sex is one that is mutually consented for a time to devote ourselves to prayer.* Clearly this is not what is going on with Janey. Perhaps, she should ask Todd for a night of prayer and abstinence until her heart is in the right place. She should then make sure that she reunites with Todd and comes together as a couple sexually *so that Satan will not tempt us because of lack of self-control.* The quickest way to push your man away is to dismiss him sexually. She is already paving the way for the enemy to open the door for Todd to sin against her. We don't want our spouse to have any motive to switch teams.

Playbook for Janey:

1 Corinthians 13:4–5 NIV, Proverbs 15:1 NIV, Proverbs 21:19 NLT, 1 Corinthians 7:5 NIV

Switching Teams

Pain is temporary. Quitting lasts forever.
-Lance Armstrong

History: His Story and Her Story

Her Story

I spent almost ten years living a lie. Thinking that if I tried hard enough, connived and plotted, I could attain my fantasy. I coveted another woman's life and set out to make it my own. It's interesting how this fantasy came about. I had a "great life" going. I was married to a handsome guy who was ready to set the world on fire. He loved money, status, and buying me expensive gifts. We had the nice home, expensive cars, jewelry, and boat. We even had a decent sex life. I also had a high-paying, challenging career. I successfully won awards and promotions. But I wanted something more, and I couldn't have it. I wanted a child and to be a stay-at-home mom. This might sound corny or old-fashioned, but once I found something I couldn't have, I wanted it all the more.

When you have the things that everyone else wants, it just gets boring. I figured if I couldn't have what I wanted, I'd start a new life. I'd create a secret world of my own. That little thought was the beginning of the end of my marriage . . .

His Story

I can't remember not wanting to get married and have kids. I always wanted three. I married the first girl I had a serious relationship with right after college. Within one year we had a little girl. Then another girl and then a boy. I got fired, got a better job, with promise of a decent salary and promotions. I got my MBA while my kids were still in diapers. I got promoted—twice. I was riding a nice high. Then my mind started to wander. Is this all there is? Married with children and letting my in-laws orchestrate every vacation and holiday? Where's the girl I used to know? Is she still inside there somewhere, or is she just as bored as me? I spent a lot of time telling everyone how great my life was, but I didn't know where I was going. Doubt crept in. I started feeling smothered by my "great life." I chose to escape . . .

These are the thoughts that some people never have or won't admit. You're married for a while, and then all of a sudden, you feel stuck in a rut. You don't know who you are, and you look at your partner and wonder where they went. In today's culture, many people will tell you that you're going through a phase.

When you start to lose your connection to someone, you become disillusioned and depressed. Your soul yearns for more. This is the danger zone. It used to be the seven-year-itch. Nowadays, the itch starts earlier and earlier.

This is what we call falling into a pit. You don't know you're going to fall. You start walking closer and closer to the edge. You feel the ground loosening under your feet, but you allow yourself to keep going closer and closer. You are testing your own strength but are unable to see you are not strong at all. You've allowed yourself to be compromised as soon as you entertain thoughts of the dreaded "D" word. Once you entertain thoughts of a life without your spouse, you need to get your head back in the game. If you don't respond to the warnings, you may find yourself alone.

When situations present themselves or bad things happen, it is easy to become angry or discouraged. In my sophomore year of high school, our football team lost nine games in a row. It seemed like we couldn't do anything right. We never even got a lucky break. As a cheerleader, you are not supposed to cry on the field, but I remember tears stinging my eyes while singing our alma mater at the end of the last game. I recall that same feeling with the Miami Dolphins in California after losing our second Super Bowl in two years. After that second loss, I was ready to quit.

We are a nation of quitters. Is this true? When was the last time you went to a movie to see the hero give up? You wouldn't want to see Batman waving a white flag and allowing the Joker to win. You definitely don't want the bad guy to get the girl.

If we don't like quitters, why do we like quitting?

Maybe we don't like it as much as we identify with it. Popular opinion says, "If you stop doing something you don't enjoy, it's not quitting. It's making better use of your time." Maybe. Maybe not. Do you enjoy every task you do in a day? Do you enjoy housework? Exercising? Working at your job? Rubbing your spouse's feet? We have to admit there are some things that need doing that aren't enjoyable.

I really prefer not to clean the toilet. However, I enjoy having the toilet clean; therefore, I do it. I have to do something I dislike to get a positive result. Most running backs don't like colliding with defensive linemen twice their size. They don't like being at the bottom of a pile of five tacklers. No matter how hard they are hit, they try their best to pop up and run back to the huddle. Quitting is not an option.

Most of us have quit an extracurricular activity in our lives. Remember piano or guitar lessons. You thought you were going to be a big star someday, but you quit after boredom set in. How long did you stick with that? What does all this trying and quitting say about us? If we grow up trying and quitting as children, what happens when we become adults?

Quitting a marriage is a much bigger decision than playing an instrument. Make every effort to avoid it. Although many have quit on marriage according to the statistics, you don't have to fall into that category. The number one reason for splitting is irreconcilable differences.

What differences cannot be reconciled? *"With God all things are possible."* [24] The desire to quit may creep in when we don't seek God's opinion. Before we embark on a new venture or activity, we should seek God's will to lead us. God wants involvement in every aspect of our lives. We get married in a church to ask for God's blessing. On the next morning and every morning, we need to ask again for God's blessing and guidance. We must remember to seek God in all things.

I recall my first wedding. I had dated my boyfriend for over a year, I was twenty years old, and some of my girlfriends were getting married. We both had decent paying jobs, I had two years of college, and I determined it was time to move out of my parent's house. My three reasons to get married were everybody's doing it, I can afford it, and I have to get out of my parent's house. With that foundation, it is not surprising we started to have problems within six months and were divorced in a year. I don't recall praying, except in front of the priest on my wedding day.

If you are going to marry another sinner formed by different backgrounds, experiences, and wiring, pray early, and pray often. A marriage unites two unique individuals and creates a new identity for both. *"And the two shall become one flesh; so then they are no longer two, but one flesh."* [25]

When you get married, you lose your independence. This doesn't mean that you are unable to make decisions, have hobbies, and pursue different interests than your partner. It means that you hold your relationship in a higher priority than hobbies and interests. If one member of the team is missing, seldom will the game advance as desired. What if the starting quarterback is injured? It will probably impact the team's ability to win. It will certainly involve restructuring plays and players to adjust to the new quarterback.

The best teams inspire dedication from their core players. Loyalty is an important characteristic of success. If a player is constantly wondering how they would perform on another team or if the other team would give him more money, he is divided instead of devoted. A team divided will fail.

Marriage is the same way. If our attention is drawn in another direction or to another person, our marriage will inevitably be broken apart. When the team's focus is no longer on God and each other, the cord of three strands starts to unravel. When problems arise, one partner may seek comfort in another instead of going home and working on the problem.

"The grass is always greener on the other side" is enticing to a troubled spouse, but this saying is not true. The grass may appear greener until we jump over the fence and get a closer look. All grass needs to be mowed, and there's always weeds to pull. Every relationship carries unique circumstances and opportunities, both good and bad. When a spouse avoids marital problems by turning their attention to another person, the marriage has little chance to recover. Lack of attention in one area and focus on another will mask the reality of the situation.

The wide receiver's number one job is to catch the ball. If he takes his eye off the ball, he usually drops it.

The receiver looks down in anticipation of running after the catch. He loses his focus. If they don't catch the ball, they have no place to run.

When we find someone else, we take our eyes off the ball—our marriage. We allow ourselves to be attracted to a person who seems to have something our spouse is missing. This is why adultery is such a deal breaker. Many times, one of the partners is unwilling to work on the marriage because they have somewhere else to go. All they want to do is escape to the other person and leave their "problems" behind.

Troubles follow them into their new relationship. The problems were not in their spouse; they were in the mirror. The new relationship does not get a fresh start. Both partners bring a bag of emotions, insecurities, and maybe even a few kids. Imagine a player going to play his first game with a new team wearing his old team's uniform. His head may be with the new team, but he has residue from his past all over him.

When a person is thinking of switching teams, you may hear rumors of secret meetings with the new team. Infidelity starts subtly with time spent with another. It may be coffee with "a friend" or "just lunch," but when you start to scratch that itch, you want to scratch more. In Christian marriage, we must set up boundaries to protect unwanted advances from others. The secular world may not understand why a woman shouldn't go out to lunch with a man who is not her husband and vice versa. I'm not talking about three or four people from work going to lunch. I'm talking about one on one, guy and girl, alone together. This is how many affairs start—a casual lunch.

When I was a single nonbeliever, I thought of myself as a free spirit. If I was attracted to a guy, I didn't care if he was married. If a married guy was interested in me, I always told myself the same justification, "He must have problems at home." When you don't belong to Jesus, you can belong to anyone. That doesn't make you free; it makes you cheap. Our bodies were designed to be shared with our spouse and no one else. *"The two become one flesh."* [26] When we unite our bodies with one who is not our spouse, we are becoming one with them. You became "one flesh" with your spouse. Your body is reserved for that person. Sexual sin is uniting with another. You defile your wedding bed, which is against God's plan.

"Now the body is not for sexual immorality but for the Lord, and the Lord for the body. And God both raised up the Lord and will also raise us up by His power. Do you not know that your bodies are members of Christ? Shall I then take the members of Christ and make them members of a harlot? Certainly not! Or do you not know that he who is joined to a harlot is one body with her? For 'the two,' He says, 'shall become one flesh.' But he who is joined to the Lord is one spirit with Him." [27]

When we are not with our spouse, we may be tempted to touch or be touched by someone else. This is the reason to set up boundaries in marriage. An affair can start off as emotional and turn into physical. If one partner is sharing their thoughts, concerns, and dreams with another person, they are sharing an intimate exchange reserved for their marriage. Inappropriate intimacy could involve texting, e-mailing, Facebooking, or a hotel room.

If you saw two members of different teams having lunch and showing each other their playbooks, it would definitely appear inappropriate. It violates the trust of both teams. When we share details about our team with

SAME TEAM

others, we are breaking a bond. We are putting our team at risk by allowing other's entrance into our sphere of intimacy. Our sphere is composed of hopes, dreams, thoughts, ideas, and information that the team has created and shared together. We have intimate conversations and experiences shared just between the two of us. Our sphere of intimacy is special. It is reserved for two. God strengthens and defends our sphere.

"As for God, His way is perfect; The word of the LORD is proven; He is a shield to all who trust in Him."[28] Seeking Him first in every decision is what brings peace and comfort. Many times we are anxious and worried about making the wrong move. We need to know how to seek God. There is no person that can truly know your heart like God. You go to Him when you pray, worship, read His Word, and spend time with Him.

The more you seek Him, the more He will lead and show you the right way. If I had sought Him before my first marriage, I would not have married at twenty years old. I was in a state of confusion and lacked the godly wisdom to know that there were alternatives to my

174

missing happiness. What if I had let God fill that chasm back then? My life would have been different. Instead of following my feelings from relationship to relationship, I would have been on God's path for my life.

God has the power to redeem any relationship no matter how poorly it starts. Most of us want to win with as little suffering as possible. Suffering is part of every life. Quitting doesn't end the suffering. Quitting prolongs it. Enduring the hard challenges of life leads us to the prize of God's calling in life. This is the only true victory.

Everybody loves a winner. We want to be like them, but many of us are not comfortable around winners. We may like to watch them and get a glimpse into their lives, but because we can't really identify with them, we end up losing interest after a while. I used to like to read true crime books because I was curious to understand the criminal mind. I realized this fascination wasn't doing anything to make me a better person. It was just a strange curiosity that was taking up my time. I put those books down and now only read things that inspire me. I made a choice to change my thoughts and actions.

The world needs more winners—husbands and

wives that never quit, no matter what. They have stayed in the game through trials, tribulations, joy, and sadness and have overcome. Winners make positive choices to satisfy their commitments and achieve their mission. They are in constant pursuit of a goal. Overcomers are busy doing something to improve their chances of success.

The apostle Paul talks about a race to win a prize. The race is the pursuit of knowing God and living for Him. The race is long, and it is constantly moving forward. The runner does not look back. He presses on in spite of obstacles in his path. He may stumble, but he does not fall because of the preparation for his body to endure pitfalls. The prize is great and awesome. The prize is what motivates every grueling step, every bead of sweat, every aching muscle, every gasping breath. The prize is being in Heaven with the King of kings. Too many of us race for so much less.

New joys are available to us every day. We can wake up today with a new joy experiencing God's creation. We can choose to start over right now because all things become new when we become His. We can choose to believe that His plan is better than ours and decide to put on the mind of Christ to avoid those things that separate us from Him. His playbook contains all the ways to win on the Same Team.

Get back in the huddle, review your plays, remember who the enemy is, put your game face on, and win the game. You made a choice to marry. Choose to stay all in. Choose to allow God to be the Head Coach until death do you part.

The Penalty: Out of Bounds

The Play: Phil and Amy

Amy has been going to lunch with a group of people at her office. Some are single. Some are married. When she and Phil got married, they made an agreement never to be alone with someone of the opposite sex. On Friday, the group went off while Amy was finishing her report, which was due that morning. Around twelve forty-five, Joe, a new young sales rep, stopped in and casually asked Amy if she wanted to grab a quick bite at the downstairs deli. Amy felt it was harmless, grabbed her purse, and went with him. Later that night, she wanted to tell Phil about the lunch, but she decided to keep it to herself.

The next day, Joe poked his head in her office and asked for help picking out a gift for his mom. Once again, she found herself alone with Joe. She told herself that she was just being helpful, and there was nothing wrong with having a male friend.

That night at dinner, Phil asked her how her day went. She said she ran into their next-door neighbor at the gift shop. Phil said, "Who were you buying a gift for?" Amy said she was helping a coworker get a present for their mom. "Anybody I know?" asked Phil. "Actually, it's one of our new sales reps, Joe," Amy answered.

Raising his eyebrows, he asked Amy what she was doing out shopping with a guy. Amy struggled to defend herself. She explained that Joe was new in town and didn't really know anyone. She was just trying to be helpful. Phil tried to contain his hurt and anger. He reminded Amy of an affair at their church that started as "friendly" coworkers. Amy started to cry. She said, "Your rules are old-fashioned, and no one else worries about having lunch with a coworker." Phil questioned, "Lunch? Are you doing that too? How far has this relationship gone?"

Amy said, "Relationship? I knew you'd overreact. I never should have said anything in the first place!" Phil was beside himself, "So what you're saying is hiding things from me is a way to avoid responsibility for your actions." Amy said she didn't want to continue this fight. There is nothing to an innocent lunch and a trip to the store. Why should she be treated like a criminal for doing nothing wrong? Phil replied, "Are you too naïve to think this guy might be interested in you?" He picked up his keys and stormed out of the house muttering, "You just don't get it!"

Coach to Phil:

Phil needs a gut check. His marriage is being challenged. Grace is required equipment when your teammate runs in to you. He's right, but that will not mend the damage. How do you reinforce the standards in your marriage without making matters worse?

Phil and Amy agreed on the boundaries for their relationship. Upon further review, Amy clearly stepped out of bounds. Phil's grace will help her get back into the game. You can't score from out of bounds. Sometimes, when we step out of bounds, we might try to blur the boundaries or question their validity. If Phil can keep his cool, he can avoid an injury.

There is no room for anger or judgment. Phil needs to pray for grace, and then ask Amy to pray with him. We join a team to have somebody that will help us up. *For if they fall, one will lift up his companion. But woe to him who is alone when he falls, for he has no one to help him up.* As we get back on the field together, we must realize that we are on the Same Team, and we have an enemy. If your intentions are innocent, don't be naïve. Satan's intentions are to kill, steal, and destroy our marriage, our happiness, and our lives. *Therefore submit to God. Resist the devil and he will flee from you. Draw near to God and He will draw near to you.*

Amy and Phil agreed upon boundaries. Phil's anger will not help the situation. The Holy Spirit could ask Phil, *"Why are you angry? And why has your countenance fallen? If you do well, will you not be accepted? And if you do not do well, sin lies at the door. And its desire is for you, but you should rule over it."* Phil can calmly review the boundaries with Amy and remind her why they established them—to protect their marriage. Phil sets the vision. God will lift them to victory. *They shall mount up with wings like eagles.*

Playbook for Phil:

Ecclesiastes 4:10, James 4:7–8, Genesis 4:6-7, Isaiah 40:31

Coach to Amy:

Amy has definitely stepped out of bounds on this one. In marriage, it is smart to set certain boundaries, especially when it comes to members of the opposite sex. Amy made one poor decision, and now she is justifying the second one. Marriage is a chord of three strands with God as your center. Amy stepped out of bounds with Joe without Phil's knowledge and consent. She violated the boundaries she should have been guarding.

What seems innocent to Amy could be fuel for another person's gossip. What did her neighbor think when she saw her shopping with another man? What if Phil was shopping with another woman? How would Amy feel?

Jesus said, *"Therefore, whatever you want men to do to you, do also to them."* If Amy saw Phil with a woman, she would feel hurt and betrayed. She disregarded Phil's feelings and her marriage. Marriage means being one with your husband and forsaking all others. Phil comes before Joe and everyone else in her life. *An excellent wife is the crown of her husband, but she who causes shame is like rottenness in his bones.* Wives have to be conscious of their actions and how they affect their husbands.

When Amy thought to tell Phil about the lunch and decided not to, she entered the danger zone. Lies of omission build walls in your relationship. *Truth stands the test of time; lies are soon exposed. The wise woman builds her house, but the foolish pulls it down with her hands.* When you are tempted to do something that you have agreed not to do, there is always a way out. Amy could have told Joe that she appreciated the invite, but the only man she eats lunch alone with is her husband. Her actions are a witness of her godly standards. Going along with philosophies of the world because everyone is doing it is a formula for disaster. *Do not be conformed to this world, but be transformed by the renewing of your mind, that you may prove what is that good and acceptable and perfect will of God.*

Amy needs to pray for discernment and ask Phil to forgive her lack of empathy. She did not put herself in his shoes.

Playbook for Amy:

Matthew 7:12, Proverbs 12:4, Proverbs 12:19 NLT, Proverbs 14:1. Romans 12:2

Boundaries

Condition comes from hard work during practice and proper mental and moral conduct between practices.

—John Wooden

The announcer cries, "We've got ourselves a real nail-biter. Fourth and goal from the three-yard line. Folks, the game is on the line. Twenty-two seconds on the clock, the tight end goes in motion. The quarterback takes the snap and rolls right. He scrambles for his life. Smith is open in the back of the end zone. The QB breaks free and throws the ball to Smith. He makes the catch. touchdown. The crowd is going crazy. Oh no! The official from the other side is signaling 'incomplete' and pointing at the end line. He's out of bounds."

When you step over a boundary, there's consequences. We have to defend our marriage against sin. The temptation to cross a line that you and your spouse established is subtle and seductive. It starts with a little itch. You don't want to do anything that would jeopardize your marriage. You just want to scratch the itch, but a little scratch is like a little yeast. *"Don't you realize that this sin is like a little yeast that spreads through the whole batch of dough?"* [29] Sin weakens the walls of protection little by little. *"Sin lies at the door. And its desire is for you, but you should rule over it."* [30] It could start with a little white lie. If the lies continue, they get bigger, and eventually, you forget you're doing anything wrong.

Every sin, whether it's lying, bringing home a stapler from work, or infidelity starts with something small and seemingly justifiable. Unfortunately, we haven't considered the consequences. Who does this lie affect? Will they tell someone? Could I get fired for taking office supplies? Did anybody see me take it? Did he think I was interested in him because we had lunch? Is he interested in me? One thing leads to another . . .

In football, the teams have clear, well-defined

boundaries marked on the field. One toe is out, the whistle blows. The play ends immediately. Once the player goes out of bounds, they can't make any forward progress until they start again—in bounds. God was adamant with the Israelites regarding boundary markers. He promised a curse on anyone who violated those borders. *"Cursed is anyone who moves their neighbor's boundary stone."* [31] When limits are defined, violators experience consequences.

In marriage, the couple should establish their boundaries ahead of time. Establish your stance on issues such as riding in cars, going to lunch, or being in any situation alone with someone of the opposite sex. This is not about jealousy or being a prude. It's about protecting your team.

My company assigned me to work at a trade show. As the show ended, a female coworker and I closed up our booth. As we walked back to our hotel, she started telling me about a personal issue with which she was struggling. The alarms inside my head started going off. I told her that I was not the best person to help her, but my wife was an excellent resource, and I gave her Angel's phone number. Angel and I had already discussed what to do. My response was according to our game plan.

Without boundaries, my Christian compassion could have led me into trouble. A woman struggling with her marriage could see a male friend as a perfect alternative. Angel and I don't want anyone to view either of us as the perfect spouse. We are perfect for each other and no one else. We want them to look to Christ for healing and restoration.

When we encounter situations that may be dangerous to our marriage, we must ask for God's protection. We have the Holy Spirit. He is the one saying, "You really shouldn't go to lunch with him," or "Don't ride in the car alone with her." He tries to protect us from ourselves. Our thoughts can get us into trouble because our actions start as thoughts. If we don't devote some time to binding our thoughts with prayer, we are opening ourselves up to the enemy who seeks to destroy us. Satan hates marriage—especially Christ-centered marriages. He loves to destroy as many as he can. He preys on them because he gets two for the price of one plus the kids.

We don't want our family to be collateral damage

during Satan's attacks. We have to understand his schemes and prepare for them. If you haven't already set up boundaries in your marriage, take the time to sit down with your spouse and discuss them. What is out of bounds for you?

The following is a list of boundary ideas:

- Don't have coffee or lunch alone with anyone of the opposite sex.

- Don't go out with the girls/guys after work.

- Don't drive in a car alone with a person of the opposite sex.

- Don't take separate vacations.

- Don't confide in anyone of the opposite sex.

- Don't have separate Facebook accounts.

- Don't have closed door meetings with the opposite sex.

Consider this list as a starting point for making a list that works best for your marriage. God wants our marriage to be holy. Holy means set apart. These seven are designed to make your marriage holy and durable. If your job forces you to have an exception to one of the rules, establish guidelines with your spouse ahead of time. How should you sit together? What topics are out of bounds? What's the time limit? Pray before, during, and after.

Do things that will enhance your marital relationship or as the Hippocratic Oath states, "Do no harm." Protect your marriage at all times and run from things that have the potential to threaten it. Same Team defends their players from outside obstructions.

What is the point of separate vacations unless it is a special event with your children? You married because you enjoy each other's company. Take the decision of a break from each other very seriously. Angel and I make an effort to spend as much time together as we can. If we have the opportunity for a vacation, we definitely want to be together.

The best defense is a good offense. Attack the enemy head-on with an aggressive strategy to build your team. Here is a positive spin on the seven "Don'ts":

- Have coffee or lunch with your spouse.

- Go out with your spouse after work.

- Drive with your spouse whenever possible.

- Plan romantic getaways with your spouse.

- Be courageous enough to offer counsel to a friend of the same sex.

- Use your favorite picture of the two of you as your Facebook profile.

- Get behind closed doors with your spouse.

If you spend more time on offense building your marriage, less time is required defending it. To improve our offense, we started kayaking. We both love the water and the peace of being on it. It's also a great place for a private talk. Find a hobby or activity that you both like to do together. Then make plans to do it frequently. Even if it's a walk every day after work, cooking dinner, or fishing. Plan it and do it. It will enhance your relationship.

Your true priorities are reflected in your checkbook and your calendar. Angel and I compare our calendars once a week and schedule a date night. Angel puts my important appointments and events on her calendar. She knows how to pray for me, and she helps me prepare. After experiencing the benefits, I put Angel's important dates on my calendar too.

Creating boundaries is for the whole family. Speak to your children and explain the importance of boundaries to them in terms of decisions, actions, and consequences. Andy Stanley asks, "Where's this going?" Kids often answer, "It's not going anywhere." He corrects, "It's always going somewhere." Our actions have consequences. It's not always negative. During a family meeting, I was firmly explaining consequences. Our four-year-old son asked, "Dad, do you know what the consequences are for loving you?" I said, "No." He said, "A hug."

A reality TV producer approached us to be on one of their episodes. She showed up to interview us during the Super Bowl. This violated several boundaries according to me and my son, Jake. After several interviews and piles of legal documents, we were chosen to be on their show. They were going to send two rebellious teenagers to live with us for two weeks. We hoped to have a positive impact on the visiting teens. With cameras rolling around the clock, would we lose our cool on national television?

We posed this question to our kids in a family meeting. Our kids were excited to be on TV. We discussed the premise of the show. We have all seen reality TV. If there is no drama, they seem to create it.

We did not want to bring unnecessary drama into our family. God promises us peace. Jesus will protect our hearts and minds from anxiety. Our boundaries would not allow us to invite unrest into our house. This would violate the protection that we established for our home.

We declined.

Boundaries are a strong defense against attacks and mistakes. Take the time to develop healthy boundaries for your home team. Establish them for home games (at home) and away games (at work and in public). This will position your team to avoid unnecessary setbacks on the road to victory.

The Penalty: Roughing the Passer

The Play: Dave and Claire

It's the end of the month and production is down from last month. Dave knows the company expects management to work late every night and Saturdays until the situation improves. Nobody has asked Dave to work late, but he assures Claire, his wife, that the bosses are watching. If she wants to move into a house some day, he has to work harder and longer than the other managers in his department. Claire has been struggling at home with her boys, Kyle, 4, and Brandon, 2. She loves her boys, but they are a handful. Claire asked Dave if all the extra hours are helping him catch up because she could sure use him at home. Dave shunned her question and walked toward the bedroom. It was now 9:30 pm. Claire had gotten the boys in bed at seven thirty. Thunder woke them at eight fifteen. Now Daddy's voice awoke them again as he had just hung up on a late phone call from one of his reps. The boys burst into the master bedroom. Dave hugged them and turned to Claire, "Honey, can you please put them back in their room? I have some e-mails to answer before I go to bed. Claire snapped, "E-mails? What have you been doing at work that you have to be up all hours working at home? When I spoke to you earlier, you said you would be home by seven, and you've done nothing but work since you got home. I'd like to see the memo that requires you to work fifteen hours a day, when we need you here not only in body but in mind and spirit." Dave was beside himself with anger. He thought Claire had some nerve attacking him after working through lunch and busting his butt for her and the boys so she could stay home. Then he shouted, "You get to stay home all day while I work for us to get the house you're dreaming about, and this attack is the thanks I get." Claire picked up the boys and sped down the hall to their room. She put them back to sleep for the third time and then snuggled with Kyle and slept in his bed all night. Dave didn't notice she was missing until morning. He got ready for work and left early without a word to or from Claire.

Coach to Dave:

Dave is working for the American dream. Is he working to please God? Dave has to be honest with himself and do everything he can to help the company, but that does not mean spending every waking moment at work. Dave is just as responsible for productivity at home as he is at work. His home team is suffering from neglect. Boundaries will help. Dave needs to reevaluate every minute after five o'clock and determine where each one is best spent. In football, good coaches make wise use of the clock. There will always be more work to do. Will Dave work through the boys' baseball games, birthdays, and his anniversary?

If he does not call on God for balance, he is headed for trouble. *There is a way that seems right to a man, but its end is the way of death.* Instead of relying on extra hours and getting the boss's attention, Dave should *trust in the Lord with all his heart* whether it makes sense or not. Give credit to God for everything and *He will direct Dave's steps.* If Dave works as unto the Lord, the Lord will help him balance family and work. As men, we cannot use our role as provider as an excuse to neglect our role as team captain. You cannot captain your team if you are not there. Dave needs time to invest in his boys *to teach his children the right path, so when they are older, they will remain upon it.* Dave needs to be diligent to know the state of his team and *commit his actions to the Lord, then his plans will succeed.* God wants Dave to work hard, get done, and go home. If he allows work to continuously encroach upon his family, he may gain a house but lose a home.

Playbook for Dave:

Proverbs 14:12, Proverbs 3:5–6, Proverbs 22:6, Proverbs 16:3 NLT

Coach to Claire:

Claire is feeling burnt out and frustrated as a stay-at-home mom. Instead of being thankful she doesn't have to go to an office every day, she is putting all her focus on Dave not being there for her. She should be thankful that he confides his concerns about work to her. Many wives beg their husbands to share their work issues with them. Although, she may be stressed taking care of two energetic boys, her job is one that can be managed with a little creativity by keeping the boys on a routine with their eating and sleeping schedule.

Claire is consumed with her problems in her world of housekeeping and child rearing and not on Dave. When Dave finally arrives home, she lashes out in frustration without considering his feelings or energy level. *A backbiting tongue brings an angry countenance,* and Claire has succeeded in provoking Dave to anger. After what he's gone through all day, this is not what he needs to hear from her. *A quarrelsome wife is like the dripping of a leaky roof in a rainstorm.*

When Dave puts in extra hours for his family with the hopes of buying a house for them, Claire's complaining wounds his ego. *If we reward evil for good, evil will not depart from our house.* How can Claire change her attitude toward Dave and his job? Is it necessary to have a new house at the expense of their marriage? It could be time for Dave and Claire to reassess their goals. Whose will are they following?

It is also time for Claire to ask Dave to forgive her sarcastic remarks. In marriage, we must *get rid of all bitterness, rage, and anger and instead be kind to one another.* We cannot expect our husbands to fulfill our every need. Claire's fulfillment can only be found in the Holy Spirit. Only God can fill us. He will never disappoint us.

By shifting our focus to helping our spouse, it will prevent us from becoming self-absorbed. Claire should *not allow the sun to go down on her anger* by sleeping in Kyle's room, thus *allowing the devil entry* to their home. *A wise woman builds her house, but the foolish one tears hers down with her own hands.* As head cheerleader of the Same Team, we must inspire and encourage.

Playbook for Claire:

Proverbs 25:23, Proverbs 19:13 NIV, Proverbs 17:13, Ephesians 4:31–32 NLT, Ephesians 4:26, Proverbs 14:1

Celebrations and Victory

Win together now, and we walk together forever.
—Fred Shero

"Hey, Mr. MVP, you just won the Super Bowl. Now what are you going to do?" As he passes by on the way to the stage, he replies "I'm going to Disney!" The whole team is on the podium crowding the owners and the coaches. The Vince Lombardi trophy is presented to the owner, the coach, the MVP, and then every single player spends time with it. Some players look like they know exactly what to do. Others look confused.

Victory is promised to every Christian. Some look like they know it. Others look like they forgot. The promise is true in every part of our life. Marriage is a powerful illustration of God's relationship with His Son and His Son's relationship with each of us. God is able. The promise is proven. Victory is imminent. Let's celebrate.

Touchdown dances become more extravagant every season. Some of them are very entertaining. Some are ridiculous. In my favorite celebration, the player enters the end zone and tosses the ball to the referee. He acts as if he's been there before, and he will be back soon. As he returns to his team on the sidelines, he celebrates with the teammates that made the touchdown possible. They bump fists and chests. They high-five.

Simple celebrations need to be frequent. High fives, fist bumps, and pats on the butt are everyday occurrences for a strong home team. Big celebrations are important for big achievements. Every day, the little celebrations keep the momentum.

Winning is fun! Everyone wants to be on the winning team. Victory is sweeter when you had to fight for it. Wins come in many shapes and sizes. Whatever challenges you have experienced, winning puts you in a positive spirit. You fight the good fight. You never give up. Your team wins.

Marriage goes through many seasons. Some seasons

are challenging. We forget the second half of our wedding vows: for poorer, in sickness, and for worse. We hope these things won't come, but they do. You have to stay together through these situations to be victorious.

The team knows that losses, injuries, and trades are part of the business. They expect them, and they prepare for them. Sometimes players are traded and new players join the team. Although the uniforms, the home field, and the name of the team have not changed, the attitudes in the locker room and the performance during the game can be night and day from one season to the next.

A couple goes from newlyweds to parents to empty nesters. Your extended family will change. The constants are God, you, and your spouse. The playbook is the same, and the Lord is with us until death do us part.

"The Lord knows how to rescue the godly from trials." [32] And His promise is to never leave or forsake us. The team should celebrate knowing that every time we stumble, He is there to pick us up. Every time we fall, He will lift us. Your spouse is not your savior. Jesus is.

With each new season of marriage you need to review the films of the past and plan for the future. Review what worked for your team and what can be improved for next season. Anniversary getaways are a great time for this reflection. Take a trip together without the kids and talk to each other. Your dreams may change. You may have learned something about yourself that you haven't shared with your spouse. Use this time together to get ready for the next season. Spend time in thanksgiving to God.

Remember all the time you spent planning your wedding day? Invest the same time and effort planning your life together from this day to forever. Track your progress by journaling, list bible studies you've attended, books you've read, tapes to which you've listened. Pictures, journals, and family traditions are ways to continue bonding your team. Create your family legacy. The team works hard every season to get better. Make every year a Super Bowl season.

Review your mission statement every year. It stays the same as your life changes. You can always rework your game plan. Make a list of what you will do this year as a couple. How are you going to stay active and healthy? What small groups will you attend? What will you do for leisure activity? Do you need a makeover? Are you still in the game?

Read 1 Corinthians 13 together and remind yourselves what love is all about. Pray together for your marriage and praise God for what He has given you. When we view love through God's eyes, He reveals truth to us through His Holy Spirit. The Spirit is the power that enables us to keep no record of wrongs, to bear all things, believe all things, hope all things, and know love never fails. Marriage is bigger than the players because the power behind the team is greater than the one in the world. God wins!

A few years ago, Mike lost his job, we became entangled in a legal matter, my dad was at the end stage of Alzheimer's, and I was hospitalized with a life-threatening abdominal attack. I realized I am not in control of my life. God is, and I can choose to trust Him or not.

Trials affect us both differently, but we are both affected. We know that when one of us is sick, the other has to help. When one of us is discouraged, the other must encourage. When one of us mourns, the other must comfort. That is marriage on the Same Team.

Every trial strengthens my faith to trust Him. When I ask God to help me, to take over my life, my marriage, my family, I remember His promise, *"All things work together for good to those who love God, to those who are the called according to His purpose."*[33] Mike encourages me with four simple sentences, "I love you. I'm not going anywhere. It's going to be OK. God's got it!"

I surrender to my Abba Father. I hear his audibles. I see answers in His word. I witness His miracles.

When Samantha, our younger daughter, was in her senior year of high school, we were praying about which college she would attend. She had narrowed her choices to two schools. When she visited the large public university, she felt like a number being processed. She was not excited; however, she would have had all of her tuition and expenses paid for by savings and scholarships. The second school was a small Christian University. They made her feel great when she visited, and the school is less than an hour away.

The choice was easy. The finances were not. The small private university was over $30,000 per year and way out of our reach. We needed a miracle. We were all together on Good Friday, and decided to fast as a family for Samantha. While we were fasting, I checked my email. I saw one from the private university but the message was confusing. I called the financial aid office for clarification. The representative started to explain in detail the aid Samantha would receive. At first, I was disappointed because each one seemed small, but as he kept naming grants, scholarships, and funds the total went higher and higher. It all added up to $29,500. With tears in my eyes, I ran into our living room where everyone was talking about our fast. I told them I had received some news already. I read off each total and the final amount as we all looked at each other's expression of joy. We received our miracle.

We have a great Head Coach. He loves both of us. He wants us to succeed. We trust Him. He loves to teach us to win. He loves to celebrate our victories. We are already looking forward to the new teams that will be birthed from ours. The spouses our children will have in their lives and the grandchildren that we hope to influence and spoil.

It's the final seconds of the fourth quarter. The ball is on the forty-yard line. The quarterback drops back to throw a bomb, a Hail Mary—knowing that a win will only come through divine intervention. I'd prefer to call it an Our Father. The receiver is battling his opponent for position as they stride toward the goal. The enemy jumps up a second too soon. The ball floats over his outstretched hands. The receiver sacrifices his body as he dives into the end zone. He is able to catch the ball with only the tips of his fingers. The announcer exalts, "What a catch!" The Same Team scores. Victory is yours!

Our prayer is for all of us to remain on the Same Team, being like-minded, having the same love, being one in purpose and in Spirit for God's glory in the next game.

Endnotes

1. Ecclesiastes 4:12, NIV
2. Genesis 2:18
3. Deuteronomy 6:7–8 NIV
4. Ephesians 4:26
5. Genesis 2:18
6. Philippians 4:8 NIV
7. Ephesians 4:31–32 NLT
8. Psalm 4:4
9. Ephesians 4:27 NIV
10. Ephesians 4:29 NIV
11. Proverbs 10:19
12. Proverbs 17:28
13. Matthew 6:19–21
14. Matthew 25:14–21 NIV
15. Matthew 25: 26–29 NLT
16. 2 Thessalonians 3:10
17. 1 Timothy 5:8
18. Isaiah 58:7 NIV
19. 2 Corinthians 9:6–8 NIV
20. Malachi 3:10 NIV
21. Hebrews 13:4
22. 1 Corinthians 7:4
23. 1 Corinthians 7:5
24. Matthew 19:26
25. Mark 10:8
26. Genesis 2:24
27. 1 Corinthians 6:13b–17
28. Psalm 18:30
29. 1 Corinthians 5:6 NLT
30. Genesis 4:7
31. Deuteronomy 27:17 NIV
32. 2 Peter 2:9
33. Romans 8:28